D1564582

The Last Good Freudian

The Last Good Freudian

by

Brenda Webster

HM
HOLMES & MEIER
New York / London

Published in the United States of America 2000 by
Holmes & Meier Publishers, Inc.
160 Broadway New York, NY 10038

This book has been printed on acid-free paper.

Library of Congress Cataloging-in-Publication Data

Webster, Brenda S.
  The last good Freudian / by Brenda Webster.
    p.cm.
  ISBN 0-8419-1395-1 (acid-free paper)
    1. Webster, Brenda S.—Family. 2. Webster, Brenda S.—Childhood and youth. 3.
Novelist, American—20th century—Biography. 4. Psychoanalysis—United States—
History—20th century. 5. Freud, Sigmund, 1856-1939—Influence. 6. Critics—United
States—Biography. 7. Jewish families—United States. 8. Psychoanalysis
and literature. I. Title.

PS3573.E255 Z465 2000
813'.54—dc21
[B]   00-020442

Manufactured in the United States of America

To Ira

Acknowledgments

I want to thank friends, colleagues, and family who have read the book and encouraged me in many ways: Carol Cosman; Marilyn Fabe; Lisa Appignanesi; John Forrester; Monica Holmes; Judith Johnson; Hannelore Schwabacher; Marcia Cavell; and Lisa, Rebecca, and Michael Webster. Alan Rinzler, Jayne Walker, and Tom Jenks provided invaluable help, as did Frederick Crews who helped me to clarify my position on various crucial points. And thanks once again to Ira who read and reread the manuscript in every phase of its development and gave me unfailing support.

The Last Good Freudian

Chapter

1

... No other system of thought in modern times, except the great religions, has been adopted by so many people as a systematic interpretation of individual behavior. Consequently, to those who have no other belief, Freudianism sometimes serves as a philosophy of life. —ALFRED KAZIN

I was born and brought up to be in psychoanalysis and, as a result, much of my adult life was spent on the couch. My family lived on New York's Upper East Side during the rich yeasty time, filled with new ideas and movements, after World War II. My father, Wolf Schwabacher, was a prominent entertainment lawyer. Dorothy Parker and her circle were social acquaintances, and his clients included playwright Lillian Hellman, said to lie even when she said "and" or "but," and Erskine Caldwell, whose novel sparked an obscenity trial that was pure theater. As a young man, my father had a bohemian side: he was engaged eight times and once popped up naked from under a table at a Marx Brothers party. My mother, Ethel Schwabacher, was a protégée of Arshile Gorky, and after he hanged himself from the rafters of his barn she became his first biographer. Later she was recognized as an important Abstract Expressionist painter in her own right, one of the very few women in the movement. My parents were idealistic, acculturated Jews, and glamorous (so glamorous that it was hard not to feel like an ugly duckling born into a family of swans).

But in addition to her beauty and her passionate love for my father, my mother brought into the marriage a serious history of mental instability in her family. Her brother was psychotic and her mother, while not obviously crazy, was frantic with anxiety and sought analytic help. My grandmother's need to be propped up emotionally was a burden to my mother, who became similarly intrusive and demanding toward me.

By the time I appeared in 1936 my mother had already had two analyses, setting up a family pattern of submission to analytic authority which made me run back to my analyst after every crisis, and kept me there, trying so hard to be "good" that it would be laughable if not for the years of pain and wasted opportunity.

Because I came from such a privileged family, the analysts who surrounded us were only the best. Ruth Mack Brunswick, one of Freud's inner circle, and a family friend, analyzed the Wolfman, Freud's famous patient who was supposedly driven mad by the sight of his parents copulating like dogs; Dr. Marianne Kris, Mother's analyst for thirty unconscionable years, analyzed Marilyn Monroe; and my own analyst, Kurt Eissler, a passionately intellectual German Jew who worshipped Freud, was the founder of the Freud Archives. They were the first wave of Freud's disciples to come to New York—many of them refugees from Hitler. They created a powerful Freudian orthodoxy and represented the cream of the American psychoanalytic elite at the height of its power. In a short time, their beliefs permeated American culture and, for as far back as I can remember, my sense of home.

My earliest memories are filtered through my mother's psychoanalytic lens. She liked to recall her favorite incidents from my childhood and delightedly repeat them to me over the years.

My own first memory, when I am five years old, is of her standing by the window in a pale peach silk kimono, covered with exotic birds. Her stomach is flat. She is thin and beautiful again.

"If Grandma loves the baby so much," I tell her, "let's cut him up and send him to her as a present."

My mother doesn't raise an eyebrow. She doesn't take me in her arms and hug me or say she loves me. She tells me it is natural to be jealous, to hate my new brother, even to want to kill him. He is guarded by a white starched nurse. I am never allowed to be alone with him, to hold him.

My next "memory" is of stealing his nursing bottle and running down the long, thin, hallway of our New York apartment, the nurse in hot pursuit.

By the age of six, I knew myself as a potential murderer and a convicted thief, an envious and jealous child—destined, like the other women in my family, for the analyst's couch.

My parents' friends, their conversation, their whole way of looking at the world, were steeped in the culture of psychoanalysis. My family's involvement spans seventy years and covers the major part of the movement's history, from its beginning after World War I, the heady days when it was associated with revolution and change, to the time when it became rigid and hostile to new ideas. When I went to my first child therapist at the age of fourteen, it was the 1950s, the golden days of psychoanalysis. Everyone in New York was going or had gone. But it was also a reactionary time, particularly for women, and analysis, at least in my case, fed into the middle-class status quo.

Freud came to America in 1909 on a lecture tour, but it wasn't until after World War I that analysis began to catch on. It got a big boost when the "talking cure" was used with shell-shocked soldiers and worked better than the previous brutal methods in getting them back to the front. After the war, adventurous bohemians and intellectuals began to try it out. For them, analysis meant sexual liberation, free love, freedom from constraints. At that time, a typical analysis could be over in a matter of months, your fixation located —mother fixation was especially popular—and your psychic energy freed. Men left their wives and went to live in the Village; the first novels about analysis (Lewisohn's *The Island Within* and Floyd Dell's *Moon Calf*) were written. It was a unique moment for a unique group of people.

My mother's family was ripe for a new faith. My maternal grandmother was an Oppenheimer, a member of an old German-Jewish banking family. Mother's family tree stretched back to the seventeenth century when an ancestor financed the Kaisers' wars. In more recent incarnations, the Oppenheimers were diamond merchants and theater owners. They were completely assimilated, leaving their children with an ideological vacuum. In succeeding generations family members divided between an attraction to Marxist-Leninism and a belief in psychoanalysis, with a hard core keeping their faith in the sanctity of money.

3

My mother grew up in Pelham, an exclusive suburb outside New York. The household included nine servants and the banquets her parents gave were so lavish that she remembered sometimes being sick after them. My grandfather Eugene ate steak and ale for breakfast and took my grandmother to German spas. It was a world of prosperity and seeming well-being. But in the early 1920s, my mother's brother James, a brilliant mathematician, became mentally ill.

I didn't learn of my Uncle James's existence until I was in college. For years, Mother kept silent about her brother. When I was a child, photo albums with his picture were hidden away. My grandmother wasn't allowed to speak his name. His psychosis was a dark secret at the center of our family. Mother was terrified that madness and genius went together, that she was crazy too, that bad blood would be communicated to her family.

James's early symptoms were largely denied by my grandparents. When Mother was in her seventies she told me that when they were children James had climbed in her bed to molest her. When she ran to her parents for help, she said, she was told to go back to bed and stop making such a silly fuss. They simply didn't believe her.

Ignoring what James did with outsiders was more difficult. He got into trouble—family stories differ as to whether he hurt a fellow student or simply acted increasingly bizarre—and was asked to leave school. By the time James had his first breakdown, my grandfather was dead. The task of getting her brother help fell to my mother, then in her early twenties.

Though James went on to get a Ph.D. in engineering from MIT, married, and had a child, subsequent breakdowns led to his being permanently hospitalized. In the meantime, Mother found an analyst for herself, Dr. Bernard Gluck, who worked as a criminologist at Sing Sing in addition to maintaining a private practice. By 1925, he was treating Grandma as well.

Grandfather would have been appalled by this development. I can't imagine him taking to newfangled ideas. He was a Southern Jew, an archetypal Victorian gentleman, a lawyer by profession, a scholar by inclination. His letters to my grandmother show him tenderly protective of her. As Grandma said later, he felt himself the guardian of the honor of any woman entrusted to him. At the same time, he felt entitled to make the most of his own freedom. For years he had fooled around with the nursemaids, even—according to Mother's reconstruction in her own analysis—getting my mother's nurse pregnant.

After his death, my grandmother was ready for liberation. She had suffered during her husband's long bout with stomach cancer and had resented his philandering. Maybe Grandma thought she could experiment and live a little. Her aging parents and her authoritarian brother, George, might have restrained her, but she had already distanced herself from her family by marrying a scholar/lawyer and by letting my mother study art. After my grandfather's death she threw herself into a variety of beliefs and practices: mesmerism, spiritualism, Christian Science, and psychoanalysis.

I suspect my grandmother saw the psychoanalyst somewhat as an ultrapermissive "Dear Abby." In her library, stuck between a French romance and a biography of Mary Baker Eddy, is a book titled *Psychoanalysis and Love* by André Tridon, one of Freud's first popularizers. A Frenchman who was captivated by the liberating aspect of Freud's ideas, Tridon gilded his toenails and gave talks in salons on topics like "Is Free Love Possible?" At one particularly shocking "psychic tea," the ladies were urged by their chairwoman to throw off their corsets "so they could learn wonderful things." Even in those revolutionary days, Tridon worried the more serious medical analysts with his amoral descriptions of men as "rutting animals" and his assertion that plentiful sex was absolutely necessary to health. Grandma marked the page in his book subtitled "getting even": affairs as a means of restoring self-confidence.

All her enthusiasms were antidotes to her pain, as well as attempts to find some authority to supersede her husband's. In the late 1920s, Grandma was remarried to a seductive German named Willy and, when the marriage ended soon after, she settled for Christian Science. Perhaps it best suited her inclination to deny reality.

By the time I began to visit her as a little girl, Grandma was an old lady in a wheelchair, paralyzed from the waist down by a stroke, living with a companion in a drab New York hotel, banished there by my mother for deeds I was only to learn about many years later. As I leaf through letters she wrote to her analyst, Dr. Gluck, in 1925 when she was middle-aged, I find her vibrantly alive—a woman who was highly interested in sex and intensely worried about it. Her manner to the doctor is slightly reticent but at the same time daring—the meeting place of Victorian Woman and something totally new that is going to push her off her pedestal.

"Dear Doctor, what would you have me do?" she writes after he has urged her to be calm about the possible loss of her lover. "It isn't easy for a sentimentalist to lose a lover at fortyfive. The pangs aren't as great as at twentyfive, but there is less hope of a successor."

Since Grandpa's death, Grandma had been hanging around with bohemians and intellectuals. The young lover referred to in the letter was a Scot named John McKay. Grandma undoubtedly imagined that John McKay, being young, would be suitably dependent and grateful to her for her largesse. But it didn't work out that way. He was socially ambitious, and while Grandma was helping him out with money and bestowing her favors, he was looking for a well-connected—and undoubtedly virginal—bride. Grandma was desperate for advice on how to hold on to him.

She thought her problem was sexual—the inhibition she'd been reading about in Tridon: "Am I one of those rare freaks, a frigid woman, or am I merely unfortunate?" she asked the doctor. "John has repeatedly asked me why I am so cold and unresponsive, then called me insatiable and said it would take a Hercules to satisfy me."

Reading over her letters, I discover something besides a remarkable openness. There is a propensity for drama, an ear for the arresting phrase, a liking for questions, an ironic humor—qualities that in other circumstances might have made a novelist. Not only my connection with analysis but my future as a writer clearly starts with her.

My grandmother used her relationship to the doctor as a spur to making at least part of her life into a story, a sort of epistolary romance. Excited by male attention, Grandma played games of withholding and teasing. Looking back, I have to admit that Grandma's dependency on the feminine arts to secure love was handed down to mother and me—all of us employed these arts, but not always to our advantage. In Grandma's case, she wanted the doctor's help, but she didn't want to ask for an interview because she was afraid to tell him exactly what she was up to sexually. I wonder how many times she actually saw him: whether in fact much of her "treatment" took place by letter.

"John asked me down to the little studio he rented from me," she writes Dr. Gluck:

> Was I a fool not to have seen he was drunk? I went with a hastily assembled supper and he was so grateful—like a child, heartily not greedily—and I couldn't resist making much of him . . . and when it was time to go, I put out the light for him and then it seemed so nice to sit there with him a moment in the dark and he asked if I loved him and I asked . . . and oh, Dear Doctor, it is so hard and I thought of the girl on the bureau top [photos a girlfriend sent John] and was alive with jealousy, and, because of that wanted to prove that he desired me.
>
> He said it wasn't fair of me to start things and then say I was going home and I asked what he wanted and he said, I must talk to you about that, there's more than one way of helping me. His way was not a nice way. I can't tell you. (I once heard of an Italian pervert who so mistreated an innocent girl. Queer what stories nice women tell other women.) I felt base, vile, and abused. That's the clue. I want to be abused and John wants revenge on his mother. His last words were, "Oh my god," and he hid his face under the blankets. I realized that I make it impossible for him not to insult me. That I love him most when he treats me worst. If I could make him respect me I could cancel that old score which since my baby days has made me court disgrace and punishment as my due.

Later, she enlarged on the theme of punishment, asked why she loved pain more than pleasure. It is a major question for the women of my family. Grandma probably felt unworthy of love very early. Her mother, Grandma Op, a great beauty with arched dark brows and a voluptuous figure, was cold and imperious. Photos show her looking down as if from a great height. Grandma Op treated her daughter Agnes, with her flat chest and curly hair ("kinky," Grandma Op called it), as an ugly duckling. Later, when my mother was a child and already clearly a beauty, Grandma Op would openly prefer her to Agnes, giving her special family jewels. In fact, however, Grandma was beautiful. Her portrait on her wedding day at the Gotham Hotel shows her in a silk and lace dress cut to display her attractively round neck and full shoulders and unbelievably small waist. Her face is oval, and nicely shaped. Short hair curling out from her head balances the tapering lower part of her face. She has lovely eyes set off by arched dark brows and a generous mouth. Perhaps her nose is a trifle too large for the taste of the day, but to me it gives her face strength. She is holding a bouquet of violets and looking at the camera with a questioning expression. Perhaps handsome is a better word than beautiful. Handsome but uneasy. Unsure of herself. Unaware of her power.

Grandma wasn't raised to think of herself seriously—she was only a girl and not considered a beauty besides—but she was talented. She was an amateur photographer and the portraits she took, especially of my mother, are wonderfully expressive. They are also extremely sensual, aware of the shock value of white skin against dark velvet or the enticement of a languid pose. I remember seeing her old bellows camera when I went to visit as a child, but I thought nothing of it. By that time, Grandma had given up portraits and spent her time crocheting afghans. These, too, showed a strong aesthetic sense—richly textured velvet yarns, daring color combinations: deep red and purple, red and brilliant orange, magenta and pale green, not old lady colors.

Mother never was explicit about her reasons for going into therapy with Dr.Gluck—her therapy began before Grandma's—but there are plenty of clues. In her journal, Mother describes at length her jealous possessiveness as a child and adolescent and her desire to be her mother's only love. Grandma's letters to their shared therapist show her, on her part, closely watching Mother's moods, alternately affectionate and critical, as when she notes that "Ethel had a crying spell. And induced me to comfort her with lavish praise. Lollipops! I suppose it's hard to teach a child brought up on superlatives, as Ethel has been, to accept sincerity."

Just as my mother later worried about the consequences of my sexuality, Grandma confided to the doctor her fears that Mother's freedom and boldness with men, though admirably sincere, would cost her her reputation. Most striking, however, is Grandma's actual meddling. She wrote to one of Mother's beaus, rebuking him for not calling her daughter when his boat docked: "No time? Piffle!" and ending, "Telephone *her* but don't mention *me*! Or write me fully and truthfully." Ignoring all reasonable boundaries, she even went so far as to tell Mother graphic details of her affair with John McKay. To Dr. Gluck, she reported: "Oh, I know you will reproach me . . . but have you ever cared enough for me to know what I feel?" My grandmother combined manipulation, coyness, and genuine distress into a lethal cocktail.

It was perhaps inevitable that Mother would think of Dr. Gluck as a sort of savior and fall desperately in love with him—it was the first example of the addictive dependency that marked her later frantic clinging to Dr. Marianne Kris during my own therapy-ridden adolescence. Dr. Gluck, Mother said, reminded her overpoweringly of her lost father. He had her father's square jaw and smoked a pipe. Just the smell of his tobacco was enough to make her feel faint.

My mother loved her father passionately. She was sickly as a child, and he coddled her, keeping her out of school until she was eight because of stomachaches. (In her later analysis, she wondered if this was the first of her neurotic attempts to get attention through illness.) Surviving letters show my grandfather, when away on business, writing to his "delicate child" with the same protective tenderness he showed to his wife Agnes. After he died, Mother sculpted a monument for him. He had been extremely patriotic, but despite his eagerness had been too old to serve in the war. Interestingly, Mother's monument to him, a series of powerful bas-reliefs, has a feminist antiwar cast. There is a woman holding a dead child, a group of women waiting, workers—all people behind the scenes. A photo shows Mother smoking a cigarette and studying this work, her velvet blouse showing between the open folds of her smock.

Mother wanted Gluck to become her lover. Given the weight of emotional baggage she brought to the request, his refusal was devastating, and she made the first of a long series of suicide attempts. Sketchbooks from late in her life contain melodramatic cartoons of herself lying on a couch in Gluck's office. Balloons over her head show that she is thinking of murdering his wife and two children. Other cartoon bubbles show bottles marked CYANIDE, or show him escaping on a plane while she is lying helpless on the floor. In one of her rare efforts to make humor out of pain, Mother nicknamed herself not Oedipus but Oedipet.

During her therapy, Mother expressed her love for Dr. Gluck by sculpting a bust of him. A photo taken by Grandma shows him as a good-looking middle-aged man, with a serious but kindly expression. Mother tried to keep on with the bust even after Gluck left the country, but couldn't stand the grief caused by contact with his image. Eventually, even modeling the clay reminded her of how she wanted to touch his skin. If her drive to be an artist hadn't been so strong she might have given up altogether at this point, but she didn't—she switched to painting. Love and loss became the major subjects of her work, and suicide her way of coping with the distress of separation.

Dr. Gluck's treatment of both mother and daughter would be unthinkable today. It certainly inflamed their rivalry, and probably exacerbated Mother's instability. When Dr. Gluck took flight to Vienna for some reanalysis, his final advice to my grandmother was to put Mother in a sanitarium.

When my mother died, I found a small notebook, which I call the rage notebook. In it there is a fantasy of cutting off John McKay's penis and shoving it down her mother's throat—choking her with her own lust. (To me this is a perfect example of how classical Freudian analysis failed to help, probably even made things worse for my mother.) She was writing this when she was nearly eighty years old, after thirty years of treatment, five days a week, still trying without success to recover some original childhood trauma, cranking out fantasies like this to oblige her analyst, stubbornly dwelling on the past.

After her suicide attempt, my mother went to Vienna, where she began analysis with Helene Deutsch, one of Freud's early followers, whose consuming interest was female masochism. Feminists have faulted Deutsch for this emphasis, without noticing that in her work she suggests that women fight a tendency to be masochistic by building up their "ego interests," their work and competence. Mother told me later that Deutsch had encouraged her painting and even found her a teacher. She said that Deutsch also cured her of her sadistic impulses toward men and enabled her to marry my father.

Deutsch's role in my mother's life didn't stop when the analysis ended. She presided over my conception like a fairy godmother. I might not have been born at all if she hadn't approved of my father when Mother took him to meet her in Boston. Though Deutsch's comment was a surprisingly lukewarm "He's all right," apparently it sufficed.

It's hard to imagine my dashing, headstrong father submitting to an audition by his fiancée's analyst. I see him arguing a case in court much as he looked in photos of that time, his dark hair smoothed down, wearing a perfectly tailored suit, gold cufflinks showing when he raised his hand to emphasize a point. People called him "the little Napoleon"—short, cocky, exuding vitality and confidence. What would have made him submit to approval this way, as though he were a horse at market?

Well, he was in love, and though he certainly hadn't been analyzed, several of his show-biz clients had tried analysis and he probably thought of himself as a very free young man. In his most famous cases, the ones he had tried just before he met Mother, he fought for the right of artists to treat sexual matters usually considered taboo. When he defended Erskine Caldwell against obscenity charges, he compared the secretary of the Society for the Suppression of Vice, John Sumner, to Hitler. When Lillian Hellman's play *The Children's Hour* was banned because of lesbian subject matter, he countersued the city of Boston for libel. In principle, he would have approved of psychoanalysis's fight against sexual repression. In practice, as a father and husband, he had something of a double standard.

In any case, going with my mother to see Deutsch set the tone for a marriage in which the emotional side of things, for better or worse, was left to her. The emotional side of things included my brother and me. She became the one to explain us to Father, and Father to us, and us to each other.

When I was born the following year, Mother took me to see Deutsch, too.

"This is your greatest creation," Deutsch told Mother warmly, moving my blanket away from my face. The signal was clear: Motherhood is woman's highest goal. Besides, according to psychoanalytic theory, having a baby is the only way a woman can get over the horror of not having a penis.

Mother loved the idea of birth. Many of her best paintings were about it, soft blues and pinks suggesting beginnings. My mother always said she would have liked to give birth to me in a field, surrounded by flowers. It was the sort of romantic, flamboyant thing she said. But the daily chores of diapers and feeding didn't appeal to her. "I didn't nurse you because Daddy was jealous," she said, flicking blame away from herself with a dismissive gesture of the wrist.

Photos show my mother, ravishingly beautiful, chiffon scarf wound around her head, holding me naked on her lap, her fingers making indentations in my baby fat. But she was hardly present. Once or twice a day she would come into the room that I shared with my German nurse and ask how things were going. The rest of the time, she painted in the corner of the living room where her easel stood.

My nurses never stayed long enough for me to have a clear memory of any of them. They were always doing something wrong and being fired by Mother. My German nurse was caught tying me to my high chair so she could force-feed me like a goose. My next nurse, an Irish girl, was fired because she let me fall off a slide in the park in 1938, when I was one and a half. I had a terrible concussion and was put to bed for six weeks. I remember Mother washing my hair in the bathtub (probably the nurse's day off). In my memory she is huge, looming over me like a giantess; my head suddenly hurts terribly and I scream. The giantess's eyes widen with alarm; I see her huge mouth open. Mother later told me I'd had convulsions and she had to force a spoon between my teeth to keep me from biting through my tongue. When I went to my first therapist at fourteen, Mother repeated the story because she thought it might have been traumatic. She also told me, proud of her acumen, that when I was finally allowed out of bed, I thought I'd forgotten how to walk. I still have nightmares of falling.

The therapist I had in my twenties remarked that perhaps my mother wished she'd spent more time with me and less with her painting. I don't think she did wish that, at least not when I was a little girl. She was probably right not to. No matter what she did, she would have been an anxious, temperamental mother. She was afraid of babies—didn't know what to do with them. Her anxiety would probably have been much worse if she had had to limit her painting.

The one thing she insisted on when she married, she told me as an adolescent, was that she should be able to continue her work. In other respects marriage changed her. She began to act more like a traditional woman. The change started even before marriage. I remember her telling me that when she visited my father at his farm in New Jersey, she was careful not to give in to his pressure to sleep with him. "I knew," she said, "he wouldn't like that." She had been metamorphosed into a virgin.

Photographs taken before her marriage show her looking seductive in a turban, smoking a cigarette with a long holder, or in velvet lounging against a wall. Photographs taken after her marriage show her to be still beautiful, but she is dressed in white painter's slacks and shirt, or after my brother's birth, in sensible tweeds, her hair wound up in a long coil behind her head. Even though it gave her headaches, my father wouldn't let her cut her hair. She was—as my father gently pointed out to me when I was slovenly or too loud—a lady.

And what about me? A portrait by the photographer, Sylvia Swami, who specialized in the children of the rich, shows me with my glossy light-brown hair cascading over one eye like a miniature movie star. Though never as glamorous as my mother, I was a pretty child with dark, expressive eyes and a full, sensual mouth—features which undoubtedly prompted the photographer's pose.

I was the perfect Freudian child; I worshiped my father. Everything about him was wonderful, from his slicked-back hair to the shiny black shoes he wore when he went out to parties. Unlike my mother, he was very physical with me, holding me on his lap, swinging me, letting me crawl into bed with him on Sundays and snuggle while he read the funnies. When I was about three, my mother explained to me in a general way that babies come from seeds, and from then on I desperately wanted my father to give me one so I could grow a baby.

Here is an early image: It's my third birthday. My father comes into my room with a big package. "For you, Bonnie," he says, crouching down next to me, so he can enjoy my happiness when I open it. "For you, princess." I lean against him for a moment smelling his skin, which has the odor of spice cookies. Then I pull off the shiny gold paper. The doll is thin and stiff with black wavy hair and has a suitcase full of beautiful dresses. I take one look and burst into tears. "But Daddy, she's too old" is all I can manage to say.

The next doll he gave me was better. She looked like a real baby and had a newly invented, rubbery skin that you could wash, and if you put water in her mouth she peed out of a small hole in her behind. A photo shows me happily naked, trying to give her a ride on the back of our Great Dane, Sero. Later, I'm told, I approached my father more directly and asked him straight out to deposit a seed somewhere—the bathroom struck me as an appropriate place—where I could gather it up and grow it. I even pointed to the exact place on the white tiled floor where I wanted him to put it. I didn't want it too near the toilet because it might slip in and be flushed away.

"Here," I said, "right here. See."

"He only laughed," my mother told me years later, "and I had to smile myself. It was so classic."

There are things that Freud was dead right about and one of them is the Family Romance. In 1941, the summer before my brother was born, I remember digging in the sand with my father. I am wearing only trunks, not the silly-looking tops the older girls wear. My hair is short. My father and I are pals. We work together from opposite ends of a big tunnel. My arm is in it up to my shoulder. My mother wouldn't be able to do this, I think. She can barely bend over now. She waddles when she walks and has to rest a lot. I feel I am gaining in my father's affections. In a photo from that summer, I have a newly confident, come-hither smile. I am slender and deeply tan. The slightly androgynous look has done nothing to diminish my allure.

My flirtatiousness attracted a host of little boys—one in particular, Johnnie, who had dark shining eyes and was always showing me how far he could jump. My father was annoyed by Johnnie's presence, digging or leaping around me. Mother pacified him by telling him—in her capacity as interpreter—how much the stocky, energetic little male resembled him. She told him he should look on it as a form of flattery.

My mother, not I, got the coveted baby. He was chubby and ugly, cried in a loud voice, and had a tiny sausage of flesh hanging down in front. Seeing my father look at my brother with the pride and affection that had up to then been all mine was shocking. Especially painful was the expression of self-congratulation and fellowship that I noticed without quite understanding. My father had produced an heir, and I had suffered my first betrayal.

Chapter

2

It is possible even for lone individuals to pit their strength successfully against the sinister forces of an unjust regime; and . . . for every gang of evil-doers who take pleasure in hurting, harming or destroying, there is always at least one "just" man or woman ready to help, rescue, and sacrifice his or her own good for fellow-beings.
—Anna Freud
From the foreword to *Code Name "Mary."*

For as long as I can remember, our lives were divided between our New York apartment on East Ninety-fourth Street and our country place, an old farm outside of Pennington, where we went for Christmas and Easter and the long, hot Jersey summers. The farm was a big one, two hundred acres set in softly rolling dairy country, surrounded by red barns and grazing cows. Everyone did what they liked there. Mother spent long hours in the fields sketching bulls and fruit trees, while my father relaxed and lolled with me by the pool. Being close to him made the farm a magical place for me as a child, and it was here, before I even knew what the word meant, that I that had my first acquaintance with a psychoanalyst.

Her name was Muriel Gardiner, a close family friend and a dedicated analyst. In 1940, she bought my uncle's share of the farm and moved in with her daughter Connie and her husband Joe, who had just gotten out of a French internment camp after heading the Austrian resistance movement during the war. Her own anti-fascist activities in wartime Europe would later make Muriel the unwitting model for "Julia" in the movie with Vanessa Redgrave.

Muriel combined a dedication to psychoanalysis with liberal politics and social-mindedness. She was a fabulously wealthy woman, heiress of a Morris and a Swift, but in college had become an anti-materialist, giving away her jewelry and furs, and involving herself deeply in political issues and women's rights.

My early memories are full of Muriel—digging out bulbs in her garden, making barbecues, or swimming naked in our pool. She always spoke to me in a frank, unself-conscious way, her mouth twitching up slightly on one side. More important, she really listened when I talked to her, whereas Mother was often preoccupied. Muriel took children's wishes and needs seriously. She didn't just talk liberation, the way my parents sometimes seemed to, she practiced it.

After my father's death when I was fourteen, I found out that Muriel had set up a $50,000 trust for me at my birth. This added to fantasies that I had about her closeness to my father—and me—despite my mother's careful explanations that the money was payment for legal services and put in that form for tax reasons.

I think I would have liked an adventurous, free woman like Muriel as my mother. As an adolescent, I wondered if she and my father had been lovers. I pictured them meeting in Greenwich Village, where she spent the summers of her analysis talking to leftists and artists in smoky bars. Instead of being brought up by a woman who was afraid of flies and thunderstorms, I imagined a mother who actually braved Nazis with guns and wondered why my father chose the way he did. The chilling thought occurred to me that it was my mother's neediness that most attracted him.

Muriel met Julian Gardiner, Connie's father, in Vienna in 1927 and married him because she wanted to have a child. She wasn't particularly fond of children, but she thought it must be one of life's great experiences. She left Julian with equal spontaneity when Connie was an infant, because she felt she could have a more passionate love.

When Connie was still a young child in Vienna, Muriel met Joseph Buttinger and helped him in the Austrian underground. Later she helped him hide from the Nazis. She didn't tell Connie that they were lovers or about the danger she was in, but Connie must have sensed the tension. She was in the middle of a war zone with a mother who was not only going to medical school and embarking on a helping profession but who was actually saving people from death. Muriel told me later that when Connie was seven she sent her with Joe on a train out of Austria.

Muriel continued to help people throughout the war, and her

house was filled with refugees. My parents explained to me that refugees were people in flight. I knew Joe was one of those refugees. Mother told me that Muriel had married him to get him out of a French camp. Joe was a stocky good-looking man with curling hair, bright blue eyes, a strong German accent and a tendency to baldness. Whatever he had done or been, I remember him, perhaps unfairly, as playing endless rounds of tennis.

Years later, when Lillian Hellman's autobiography, *Pentimento,* came out, Muriel recognized herself in Julia—Hellman's friend who worked with the underground in Vienna. Muriel, like Julia, in one of the most gripping scenes from the movie based on her story, was at the medical school when the Nazis attacked. Soon after, she began to help the resisters, saving Jews and other dissenters. She was given the code name Mary.

My brother suspected that my father must have told Lillian Hellman Muriel's story—this was later confirmed by her biographer—and Lillian simply appropriated it. Muriel, with characteristic candor, found this hard to believe and wrote to the antifascists she'd worked with in Vienna asking if another American woman was also involved in the underground. Their answer was, "Only Mary." Muriel's memoir, *Code Name "Mary,"* set the record straight.

Our house nestled against Muriel's much larger one at the end of a dirt drive flanked by overarching maples. When my brother, Chris, was born, there wasn't room for him—our house had only two bedrooms—so he and his nurse, Mrs. Sykes, were put in a nursery room adjoining the caretaker's cottage next to the barn.

Mother acted as if Chris's existence—even removed to a discreet distance—was a blow from which I would never recover. Her views demanded that I be devastated or at least green with envy. Her response was to offer me gratification from an earlier, happier time in my life, what she thought of as the "oral stage." She took me into the nearby town of Pennington for chocolate milkshakes. I remember sitting at the soda fountain counter, slurping up the sweet thick malt and feeling that somehow I'd captured her attention. My happiness was short-lived. At some point, she suggested that if I wanted to drink out of my doll's bottle that would be all right and I lay in bed at night sucking water out of the tiny unsatisfying nipple. It would be decades before I'd begin to wonder why she wanted me to do this.

Much later, after Mother told me about her brother, James, she said that she loved me best because I was her firstborn. Her mother always preferred her brother. She didn't want to do that. I was happy when she said she loved me best, but I didn't believe her. Though she was careful never to praise Chris in front of me, I couldn't help thinking she was protecting me from the fact that he was always in her thoughts. I concluded that love was in limited supply.

When Chris was around three my father began taking an intense interest in him. That was when I really started to suffer. Chris and I would be lying under the trees shading the lawn while my parents rested nearby. I'd ask Daddy if we could go biking and he'd say, "Not now, sweetheart, it's sweltering today," and then Chris would toddle over with his blue ball and whine, and my father would jump up and start rolling it to him. Chris couldn't catch it, of course, but my father would drop it in his hands and purr "Good boy" as though he had. It was infuriating and, accompanied by my mother's harping on my "envy," made me wonder if there wasn't something special about being a boy after all. I began to hate the way Chris strutted around naked like a curly-headed cherub with his penis bouncing.

Mother insisted it was natural for me to have murderous feelings towards Chris, but when I actually did something aggressive she was outraged. Once, around this time, Chris was lying in a hammock in the back of our house at the farm wrapped up in his blanket, swinging, and I began idly poking at him with a stick. All of a sudden he started to scream—I had hit his eye. When they came back from taking him to the emergency room—there was no real damage—I got a lecture about my responsibilities as the elder sister that was more shaming than a spanking.

Shortly thereafter Chris had his tonsils out at home. I felt as if it were my fault. Hadn't I wanted something to happen to him? The event itself was horrible enough. Doctors and nurses rushed into Chris's room and plumped a gas mask over his face. He didn't even have time to scream. "Tonsils are useless prongs of flesh in your throat," Mother told me. The doctors blamed Chris's tonsils for his winter-long colds. I was frightened. God only knows what mutilation they were preparing for me. Afterwards I was much sweeter to Chris. He didn't want anyone but me to feed him and I brought him Jell-O on a lacquered tray, imagining myself a nurse. When he got better, I pulled him behind me in a red wagon.

Sometimes I liked being a big sister. Taking care of Chris and showing him things could be fun as long as he acknowledged I was the boss. Chris was a cowardly, goody-goody sort of little kid— afraid of the water, of riding his trike—always pursing up his little lips in a precociously mature expression of disapproval when I did anything "bad." Nurses liked him because he was easy to care for. If you sat him on a stoop and said, "Stay," he would sit there for an hour like a well-trained dog. I thought my father would have been much better off with me as comrade-in-arms. By the time I was six or seven, I was eager to do the daring things my father liked—hunt and bicycle too fast down hills—things I associated with being a boy. My father still called me his princess and sat by my bed every night telling me stories about a daredevil cat named Katzen, but there was always the nagging fear he preferred Chris.

My ideal of what a girl could be was Connie, Muriel's daughter. Our house at the farm was under the same roof as Muriel's but with separate entrances. Downstairs was our small living room crammed with the colonial furniture my father loved. The bedrooms were up-stairs: mine, a spacious blue room, looked out on the vegetable gar-den; my parents' had the same view but it was painted pink and decorated with delicate Victorian cutouts. Next to their room a double door led to Connie's bedroom in the other house. No matter how often I did it, crossing the threshold was like stepping through Alice's looking glass.

Connie had green eyes and black hair that she cropped short like a boy's. She usually wore a pair of baggy shorts and no shirt. Her body was lean and strong, her face covered with freckles. She was a free spirit, a sort of female Huck Finn. Four years older than I was, she was allowed to do pretty much what she wanted. She had not only stripped her room of furniture, including the bed, but had filled it with rows of rat cages—except for a fenced-off por-tion of the floor that was covered with sand for her turtles. Much of the time she slept out in the barn or in the woods, where she caught more exotic creatures like skunks, who were kept in fenced runs off the barn.

"Come skunk hunting with me tonight," she would murmur seductively when I was helping her tear Kleenex for her mouse nests. "There's a full moon."

"Can't," I'd say, looking down at her bare feet crusted with dirt.

"Little sissy," she'd say in a tone that was affectionate but deeply scornful. Later that night I'd hear her yelling outside the window for Muriel to come down and pour tomato juice on her; she'd been sprayed and smelled too bad to come in the house.

I was allowed to run around and play freely, but my parents would never have allowed me to make a zoo of my room, even if I'd tried. For social occasions, I was expected to look like a little girl, with a nice dress and patent leathers (I would never have admitted to Connie that I took pleasure in such finery). Connie's animals—including a wild squirrel who bit the hired man in the groin—and her gamey room were the opposite of girlish. Though I didn't realize it then, it was extraordinary for Muriel to let her daughter grow up this way. Not only because Muriel was a woman but also because she was studying to be an analyst, and though analysis favored sexual liberation, it also believed in clear boundaries between the sexes: Men were active, women passive and envious of men.

Muriel clearly didn't accept any of this. She had been brought up with brothers, and had noticed by the time she was three that they were given more freedom; she wanted to do everything they did. None of the women she knew, she once told me with a laugh, were like Freud's typical females.

Muriel had been analyzed in Vienna by Ruth Mack Brunswick, an early follower of Freud, but from the beginning Muriel was a maverick, disputing the theory of female masochism and writing a satiric article on the docility of analytic wives. Her two courses of analysis seemed only to have made her stronger.

After analysis Muriel stayed in touch with Ruth Mack Brunswick and often invited her to visit us at the farm. Mother disliked Ruth, who, she claimed, used cocaine and demanded to be treated like visiting royalty. I don't remember her, but when I was about six, Judge Mack, Ruth's father, arrived one day in a very grand car with his friend Albert Einstein in tow and a huge basket of goodies for a luncheon alfresco. The only reason I remember this is that Einstein had an amazing head of hair and an otherworldly smile. I got to sit on his lap, and Otis, the hired man, who'd been asked to serve, was in a flurry of nerves for fear he would spill something on the great man's pants.

I was fascinated by Connie's mixture of maternal and boyish qualities. She walked oblivious through spiderwebs, caught skunks with her bare hands, and wasn't afraid even when they succeeded in spraying her with blinding scent. With her mice, though, she was tender and protective. There is nothing so helpless as a newborn mouse. They are hairless and pink like tiny piglets with shut eyes and gaping mouths. If they were motherless, she taught me how to feed them with an eyedropper and later how to fill their feed cups and change the paper without disturbing the Kleenex nests.

Connie was as passionate as any patriot—and she had an enemy too, cats. One day, I mistakenly let out some kittens that were locked in the woodshed. Connie must have been planning to have them taken away by the hired man, possibly drowned. She was furious at me—I must have been around six or seven by then. She tracked down the kittens and put them into a burlap bag. Then she made me go with her to the barn and hold the bag while she smashed their heads with the blunt side of an ax. For years I saw it in my dreams. And when I was about ten, I wrote it down, then again in high school—forgetting about it completely after each time. When I first started writing fiction again in my forties, after a long gap, my first story was about Connie.

I loved Connie. Photos from that time show me riding her around the yard like a horse. She is wearing shorts and suspenders and smiling good-naturedly.

I used to think it was simply the brutality of it that made the kitten episode haunt me. But now I think there was more. I idolized Connie, and until the kitten incident, I really wanted to be like her. But what if being active and free meant you might kill? Wasn't it better to stick to being a girlie girl? At the time, I just ran crying to my mother, who said I played with Connie too much, and let me climb into her lap.

Somehow being a girlie girl became associated in my mind with being a victim of Nazi aggression. My parents didn't talk much about the war in front of me, but by the age of eight or nine I had seen enough war posters of goose-stepping Germans and snarling Japanese soldiers to imagine monstrous cruelties. After Connie killed the kittens, my nightmares were set in the barn. Men with bayonets and guns—images picked up from the war news—hunted me, cornered me, woke me screaming with terror. In my dreams I became an escape artist. My unconscious somehow managed to set up the dream scene near a window so I could crawl out, get away. But it wasn't until I was in my forties that I was able to turn on my attacker and frighten him off.

Various analysts have commented that such dreams are typical of girls and express a fear of sexuality or of a girl's desires for sex with her father. I don't know. Certainly by the age of nine or ten my fantasies mixed violence with romance of a sort. I would imagine being kidnapped—usually from my math class, which I hated—by a gangster or gangsters who hovered above the window in a helicopter, then climbed down a rope ladder. In these fantasies, I would reason with the men, somehow converting them to good, and they would end up kneeling at my feet.

While I don't have any memories of masturbating to my fantasies, masturbation was a subject that fascinated me. Lynn, my best friend in fourth grade, had a doctor father and once she showed me a medical book that said masturbation made you crazy. Lonnie, another friend, played with herself in math class—she used to lean forward, humming, moving rhythmically up and down. The fact that Lonnie was emotionally disturbed may have added fuel to the idea that it was a dangerous activity.

Horseback riding stimulated me without my having to be aware of it. It also had an element of danger. I was always being thrown. Riding horses also brought me closer to my father. By the age of ten, I desperately wanted my own colt.

"Please, Daddy," I would beg, screwing my face up in expressions I had practiced in front of my mirror. "I know I could raise it. I could train it." I was a devotee of *Black Beauty* and *My Friend Flicka*.

"Colts are skittish creatures," he said, stroking my hair. "I don't want you to get hurt."

I didn't give up easily. I got the brilliant idea of painting a touching scene of mares with their colts. Daddy loved Mother's painting. Every day when she came out of her studio at the farm, she would show him her work and he'd murmur about how beautiful it was.

Maybe he'd love my horse painting and somehow it would persuade him to give me what I wanted.

I asked Mother for an easel of my own. In New York, she had her easel in a corner of the living room—her painting, like my tomboy-ishness, was something that had to be tidied up in front of other people. At the farm she had a studio, but it was hidden. To reach it, you went past the barn—the border of my known territory—and walked through waist-high grass until finally the studio with its green awning surprised you in a little clearing.

In 1946, she had a show coming up at the Passedoit Gallery in New York, her first solo show since my birth, and she was working hard that summer. Mother's paintings—of red and black bulls, giant lilies—had a lot to do with sex. Even her peaches hanging from dark leafy branches seemed radiant with the life force. Her mentor and friend, Arshile Gorky, was close to André Breton, whose *Surrealist Manifesto* was heavily influenced by psychoanalysis. He had discovered it during World War I when he worked as a medical orderly. Breton wrote the foreword to the catalogue for Gorky's first major show in 1945 and his literary, somewhat precious style aroused the critics' antagonism toward Gorky's work. I didn't know the theory behind Mother's art—the importance of symbolic forms, association of ideas, dream images—but I certainly sensed its vitality.

I decided to set up my new easel under the eaves in the barn where I could see the summer fields. My mother at the time considered herself a surrealist and her natural forms often transformed themselves magically by a sort of free association: The center of a peacock's tail would become an eye or a flower. But I was a realist. I wanted things to look the way they were.

My plan was to show the fields sloping gently backward toward the woods behind them and then to put in some horses. But my canvas was a disaster before I even got to the figures; my fields resembled oblong swatches piled on top of each other under a strip of sky blue. I don't know where my mother got the idea that she couldn't teach me the simple elements of perspective; when I grew up, I mastered them from a handbook in a few days. But she just kept repeating that if you tried to teach your child what you loved, she would rebel and hate it. Finally, she had pity on me and, since I couldn't do it, drew me a colt in pastel, its fur so soft I could almost feel it—a velvety nose and liquid eyes.

Instead of getting me a colt, my father bought me a fancy show horse, Brambles, a horse with a reputation for throwing adults but supposedly gentle as a lamb with children. She was a big beautiful chestnut with fine carriage. But the first time I rode her alone, she took the bit in her teeth, galloped down the road, and threw me in a ditch.

After that, I regularly ended up in ditches. I would lie in the field, not answering, while my father and the caretaker, Otis, called my name. The fear in their voices gave me a special thrill. Let them think I had broken my rib again the way I had when Chris's pony kicked me. Let them even think I was dead. I stayed hidden in the tall wheat imagining them crying at my funeral until I couldn't stand it anymore and sat up and let them see me. Then I knew with delicious certainty that my father would scoop me up in his arms and carry me back to the house.

My father eventually accepted the fact that Brambles was too much horse for me and got me a chunky, stolid black nag that I named Trigger, after Roy Rogers's horse.

Sometimes my father would ride with me in the early mornings before it got hot. I loved the fresh smell of the wet grass and the scrunching sound his boots made on the gravel, loved the way we curried our horses side by side, running the rough metal around to loosen the dead hair, laughing over their dandruff, brushing them until you could see highlights on their fat rumps, then saddling up and riding out, the horses snorting and farting and dropping piles of pleasantly steaming manure.

We watched the blacksmith shoe our horses. Sparks flying from the anvil, the sound of ringing metal, the smith's worn leather apron. The strong smells of horse. But the thing I liked best of all was when we saddle-soaped the tack at the beginning of every summer. Wiping the warm foam on the leather, rubbing it around, thinking of how the leather was drinking it in. Sitting close to my father, watching him squeeze the sponge so the bubbles of foam burst out. I usually hurried my chores, but for this one I lifted each flap, undid all the buckles on the straps, did everything to make being with him last.

I never regained the confidence I'd had as a small child that I was going to get my father all to myself. But I did have pleasant fantasies about riding off with him on some satisfying adventure. The fantasy usually ended with our bringing back a huge bear and throwing it at the feet of my astonished mother and brother. Riding together and caring for our horses didn't quite match my three-year-old wish to grow his baby, but it did create a small corner where our romance still flourished.

Chapter

3

*The neighborhood in which the [Dalton] school
is located contains some of the most costly real
estate in this country. . . . Politicians refer to it as
the "Silk Stocking" district of New York. . . . A
sense of wealth and well being is . . . underscored
by the early morning scene of white-gloved
uniformed doormen hailing taxis or opening the
doors of limousines. . . . Only a careful
observation will reveal the sign, THE DALTON
SCHOOL, placed discreetly above the . . .
entranceway (and . . . so indiscreetly displayed
by filmmaker Woody Allen in . . . Manhattan).*
—SUSAN SEMEL

*D*alton was the perfect school for me. Founded by Helen Parkhurst in the 1920s, it drew the children of intellectuals, artists, and professionals. This innovative school combined my mother's ideas about creativity and the evils of repression with my father's interest in community. My father served on the board along with other socially minded German Jews, including Stanley Isaacs, "the conscience of the New York City Council," and Benjamin Buttenweiser, a wealthy, liberal friend of Alger Hiss. Lloyd Goodrich, curator of the Whitney, was also on the board then, as were Jacques Barzun and Orville Schell senior. As a child, I remember my father saying how good it was that Dalton not only taught children independent thinking but also taught them about their social responsibilities. I doubt if he mentioned the fact that Dalton had an unusual number of Jewish students for those days. Most other independent schools excluded Jews. Dalton was also unusual in that it accepted blacks.

Dalton was founded on the ideas of the philosopher John Dewey, the father of progressive education. Though Dalton wasn't explicitly tied to psychoanalysis the way some of the new schools were, there were many points of contact between the progressive school movement and psychoanalysis.

Progressive education was born as part of a reform movement in the early twentieth century. Dewey hoped his radical new teaching methods—which stressed individual growth and social awareness—would preserve the civilized values threatened by the dislocation of migrant workers. To illustrate his ideas, he created the Laboratory School in Chicago, which taught an integrated curriculum of basic subjects and emphasized the role of experience. "Learning by doing" was Dewey's principle and Dalton's catchphrase.

Freud thought Dewey was one of the few great men of his time. They were both antitraditionalist and antirepressive. Ironically, they were equally authoritarian in their insistence on a permissive liberty.

In Dalton and the other new progressive schools of the 1920s, there was no more sitting in rigid rows absorbing facts. Spontaneity, including sexual curiosity, was encouraged and attention was given to the child's real interests. In terms of the psychoanalytic model, this could be seen as sublimating libido into intellectual pursuits rather than simply repressing it: the child's relation to learning would be more genuine and creative, drawing force from her sexuality and aggression. The social child, the future citizen, was also important, and the goal here with Dewey, as with Freud, was to replace irrationality—including prejudice—with reason.

I went to Dalton from the age of three and I always loved it. Unlike my nurses, who prized docility, the Dalton teachers praised my energy and "creativity." By the age of six I was reading and writing little stories that were printed in the Lower School paper. Mother told me years later that I never wanted to go home.

"It was horribly embarrassing," she said, drawing out the syllables. "The minute you saw me coming to pick you up, you would scream, 'No, noooo!' and run and hide." I smiled sheepishly. I couldn't say why I hadn't wanted to go home.

From the early grades we practiced Dewey's hands-on philosophy—blissfully ignorant that what we were doing went back to Jean-Jacques Rousseau's Emile and Héloïse, his ideally educated children. Like Emile we did concrete things—planted seeds, milked cows, and made model volcanoes that really exploded. We even got to tie up our teacher and do a war dance around her when we were studying the Indians. When we were in fifth grade, we observed animals feed, mate, and reproduce in our living museum. By then, we had started on world history so that we could be global citizens.

Since public schools didn't teach Asia and Europe in lower school, our teachers wrote the textbooks. (Dhan Gopal Mukerji wrote our text on India and Mrs. Seeger *The Pageant of Chinese History*.) Reading was accompanied by field trips to see ancient mummies or Greek vases, and plays wherein we imagined ourselves inside the skins of people of different races and cultures. It probably wasn't a coincidence that many of our teachers, like our third grade teacher Tess Ross, who was a Belgian socialist and disciple of Dewey, were sympathetic to the political left.

Our report cards, in line with progressive ideas about minimizing competition, stressed cooperation and effort as much as attainment. There were no tests and no grades. By Middle School (fifth grade) we were given flexible monthlong assignments in each subject (the Dalton Plan) and allowed to work out the order for ourselves. Starting in the sixth grade, I spent a lot of time writing short stories.

Flexibility and freedom were at a premium, but sometimes spontaneity was overdone. To learn grammar we sat in a circle and imagined what part of speech we would have invented first if we were cavemen. Would it have been an expletive ("Ugh") or a word to signal danger ("Look") or something on the order of "Me Tarzan, you Jane"? This was fun, but when I graduated from high school I still had no idea where to place a comma.

"Just express yourself," Gwen, our flamboyant, redheaded art teacher would say, swooping her brush in widening circles. I didn't want to express myself; I wanted to learn how to draw a horse. But when I tried to copy from a drawing book I'd brought to class, Gwen took it away. "Your paintings are beautiful," she lied. "Respect your talent."

In general our teachers walked a fine line between permitting freedom and maintaining control. They thought, like Rousseau, that children are essentially good and eager to learn. They were optimistic that if they taught us to think independently, we'd be protected from mass hysteria and fascistic movements. This was similar to the early hopes of psychoanalysts—though Freud himself was increasingly pessimistic—that wars could be prevented by analytically informed child rearing.

Sometimes the lessons backfired. To show us the evils of oppression in ancient Egypt, our fourth grade teacher made half the class pretend to be Hebrew slaves and the other half overseers, while we erected a mock pyramid. Unfortunately, it turned out that the young Egyptians—including me—liked having our slaves fetch and carry. Power was a heady experience. Needless to say, the teacher quickly canceled the exercise.

Dalton's attitude toward religion was relativistic. Mrs. Durham, the principal, had a five-foot statue of Buddha in lotus position in the hall outside her office. We sometimes put a flower in its lap before our conferences. She also had a series of eclectic festivals marking turning points in the year. At Christmas we sang carols and put on a Nativity pageant. But around the same time there was a pagan festival celebrating the winter solstice. And at graduation, we marched through a flowered arch singing our utopian school song:

> We go forth unafraid, strong with love and strong with
> learning
> New worlds will be made where we set our beacons
> burning . . .

Interestingly, none of the Jewish holidays were celebrated. That probably reflected the way Judaism had been translated into social activism for many of our parents. My father was on the boards of directors of the Baron de Hirsch Fund and the Lawyers Division of the Federation of Jewish Philanthropies. A rabbi he knew told him that though Father never attended synagogue, his fund-raising activities assured him of a place in heaven. Father used to tell us, laughing, how hard it was to get "the old Yids" to cough up some dough.

His mother was a German Lutheran who converted to Judaism when she married Grandpa David. Her lighting of candles on the Sabbath was the only Jewish religious activity I ever heard about. Certainly I had never been to a synagogue.

We celebrated Christmas with a deep green, sweet-smelling tree, brought from the farm and crowned with a gold star. There was an angel too, and balls of red and silver and cottony snow. None of it had any religious significance. It was all a glorious pagan celebration, a sort of tree worship with pies and presents thrown in. Grandma with her Christian Science faith healer was the only believer in our family.

As a child, my mother had been persuaded by her Catholic

nurse that sin and hell were realities. As an adolescent, she read Saint Augustine, ate only vegetables, and wanted to live as a mendicant. That was before she discovered the liberating doctrines of Freud.

Psychoanalysis satisfied Mother's hunger for belief. It became, in effect, our family faith. Three of her friends were analysts—one, Margaretha Ribble, had written a book called *The Rights of Infants*—and Mother consulted them about me the way an Orthodox Jew would consult a rabbi.

For a long time I thought you could choose your religion like a dress or shoes. Then once, toward the end of the war, I overheard one of the refugees Muriel Gardiner had installed in her house—a thin man with sunken eyes—describe the death camps. It must have been Christmas break because there was a roaring fire in her fireplace and people were standing or sitting on the comfortable sofa in front of it. No one saw me standing by the door. A small balding man with an intense expression and a haunted voice was telling how he had dragged corpses from the barracks to an open pit and thrown them in. Sometimes they were still alive and asked for water or a blessing, but he was too exhausted to give it. This still tormented him, he said. I ran away, horrified, and hid in the barn. That night at dinner, I told my father I didn't want to be Jewish. This was one of the few times he seemed really angry. "Well, you are," he said, "and if you'd been in Germany, you would have gone into the ovens." I bowed my head, but secretly recoiled.

My father didn't realize the vast difference between us. He'd had a mother who prayed and celebrated the Sabbath. My mother was an atheist. He grew up with a strong sense of being Jewish that he showed by his involvement in Jewish causes. But this didn't provide enough context for me to feel a Jewish identity. People we knew didn't talk about being Jewish. They didn't look for their roots in those days, and, above all, our friends didn't practice or worship together.

I missed having a faith. I longed for something with ritual and color. In sixth grade we were studying the Middle Ages and took a trip to the Cloisters in Manhattan. A nun came to speak to us; she stood shyly in front of a tapestry of a gold-haired virgin caressing a unicorn and told us about her life. I was moved by the romance of it, the contrasts of bright and dark, just as I loved the gorgeousness and solemnity of the Mass when I occasionally went with our Catholic cook, Catherine.

I developed fantasies—brought on by his insistence I wear child-like clothes—that my father would like me to retire to a convent. He kept a photo of me on his desk at the office. I was wearing a prim cotton piqué dress chastely edged with lace and was looking dreamily at the camera, hair rippling down my back. Daddy's little girl.

My progressive education raised a lot of questions that I still haven't solved: about impulse and control and the limits of freedom. Just under the surface were fears about the price of doing creative work. Mother was hysterical before her show at the Passedoit, even though afterward it seemed silly, the reviews were so good. Could being an artist drive you crazy?

In sixth grade I met Judy Johnson, a dark-haired, slender girl with burning eyes and a nervous habit of biting the inside of her cheek. In a way, Judy was my generation's version of my mother, a fiercely creative person—but without Mother's passion for psycho-analysis.

Judy's father, the distinguished Dickens scholar Edgar Johnson, had read her medieval romances as bedtime stories when she was younger, and she used to confide some of the more gruesome details of medieval torture practices to me in a hectic whisper, her voice filled with orgiastic pleasure. Though I often protected weaker children, I was sometimes cruel myself; I would exclude one of my friends, say mean things. At my worst, one summer at camp, I tormented a fat girl by mashing flies on her pillow. But I didn't have a thirst for images of cut-up flesh. I was fascinated by the way Judy, who was herself gentle to the point of passivity, dwelt on details of violence, almost as if she were looking at dirty pictures. I still remember her gleefully describing a torture where an unfortunate man was left chained while rats ate their way into his anus.

By the end of sixth grade, she'd already announced to me that she was a genius in three fields: poetry, sculpture, and music. Like Mother, who considered herself a genius born by ill-luck in the body of a woman, Judy was obsessed with genius. Her sensitivity to cruelty made her precociously sensitive to its cultural manifestations. She showed me a poem she wrote renouncing her belief in a

God so cruel that he'd ask Abraham to sacrifice his son. She was unaware that this was an adult subject, that other kids were trading cards with pictures of *Blue Boy* and *Pinkie*. I was impressed by her daring. I didn't believe in God, either, but I couldn't imagine challenging the whole Judeo-Christian tradition.

Judy's stand against God was accepted by our teachers as a rational protest, but the children thought it was weird. Her special gifts seemed to set her apart from other people. She obviously suffered, biting her nails to the quick. It wasn't easy to be a genius.

The summer after sixth grade, in July, 1948, there was a far more terrible example of what could happen to an artist. Arshile Gorky, Mother's teacher and friend, hanged himself in his glass house in Connecticut. Gorky had become Mother's teacher after her analysis with Helene Deutsch. Mother liked to tell me that as soon as she met him and saw his work, she recognized his genius just the way Gertrude Stein had heard a little bell go off in her head when she met Picasso. Mother always called Gorky "Maestro" and the word seemed to make him roughly the equivalent of a Greek god.

Mother had known for a long time that Gorky was in great emotional pain, and had arranged for him to see a psychiatrist, but he never made it to his first appointment. We were at the farm when we heard he had killed himself. I have a vivid memory of my mother crying uncontrollably, and my father trying in vain to comfort her. The memory is tinged with fear at the intensity of her grief.

What I didn't understand at the time was that Gorky had suffered a series of blows. A fire had destroyed a year's worth of paintings, cancer had destroyed his potency, his neck had been broken in an accident, and finally his wife had left him. The salient fact for me was that he was an artist and it seemed that Art, like Sex, was dangerous. From what I could make out from fragments of conversations, being an artist was like being a high-wire walker in a circus. You exposed yourself to the crowds. You were always in need of money. Unless, like my mother, you had someone strong and capable like my father to take care of you, you might just crack. Daddy gave one of Gorky's paintings to the Museum of Modern Art in 1941 and got him a grant after his operation for cancer in 1946. But even he couldn't save him from the critics who referred mockingly to his incoherent "accident pictures."

The image I associate with his death is snow, mounds of white snow backed by dark green firs. I am trying to ski down a small slope. I've never done it before and my legs open and I fall into the soft snow. Gorky helps me up. He laughs. Mother and I were at his glass house in Connecticut. It must have been the winter before he died. How black his long hair and moustache seemed against the whiteness. How big he seemed. How cold it was. I noticed his coat had patches on the elbows and that it seemed too short to cover his wrists. I remember the house itself, the huge glassed-in living room, high roof, sparse furnishings.

At some point, he began to lay paint on a canvas with a palette knife, and I wondered at its thickness. I see him standing back looking at it, black hair over his forehead, black eyes like coals. Intent. His children, Maro and Natasha, must have been there, though I remember them only vaguely. I was more impressed by the white sheepskin rug placed next to my bed upstairs in just the right place for toes to snuggle into before crawling under the covers. It also gave me a sense of being in a primitive enchanted forest with a woodcutter and his family. Gorky's wife, Agnes, was beautiful with her long black hair and blue eyes, but she was very nervous. I dimly sensed there was some trouble in the house, but no one knew Agnes was thinking about leaving. On the contrary, Mother was planning to write a book with her about Gorky. She and my father had already gone to Lloyd Goodrich, associate director of the Whitney Museum, for assurance that he would publish it. Agnes had begun to make preliminary notes.

When Gorky died, the writing project became part of my mother's process of grieving. She wrote the catalogue for the Whitney's memorial exhibit in January, 1951. I remember our house filled with Gorkys stacked up against the walls, brilliant with color and enigmatic shapes, but they couldn't cancel out the fact that Mother often sobbed while she looked at them and that Gorky had tied a length of rope around his neck and jumped. Artist or not, I thought, how could a man have purposely gone and left his children without a father? My mother kept saying analysis could have helped him—it was clear that she thought the mind doctors had great power. I had no way of judging back then, but the relation of art to madness and suicide stayed in my mind as a tantalizing puzzle whose solution could mean the difference between life and death.

Chapter

4

*[My father] had preached the liberated life and
an open mind. . . . Then, having opened so many
doors, he looked around the world and saw to
what risks he had turned me . . . exactly as the
Christian missionaries, having taught their
converts how to spell, saw with a sense of
nemesis what titles the natives chose to read.*
—ELEANOR MUNRO

Seventh grade at Dalton was the great divide between childhood
and adolescence. I began to note inconsistencies in my parents' attitudes and to pay more attention to the opinions of my peers. I imi-
tated the things they did: kept scrapbooks, danced, fussed with my
nails and hair. Though Dalton was an experimental school, most of
the girls were conventional and aimed at marriage. I quickly discovered that I wasn't good at the typical girl things: I got mascara all
over my face and couldn't seem to get my curlers in right, no matter
how hard I tried.

A photo from the time shows me in one of the little girl dresses
that my father liked, bangs, long hair flipped up at the shoulders, a
sensitive brooding expression, perhaps unhappy at being asked to
pose, one arm gracefully across the carved sofa back. Another more
casual shot shows me standing next to my father at the Cape. I am
wearing shorts. My hair is disordered, and I am smiling happily,
more comfortable as a tomboy than as a lady.

I became curious about my parents' attitudes toward sex. By the
time I was twelve, for example, I knew that when my father was
young he'd been what my classmates called a "heartthrob." One
day he brought up a barrel of old love letters from the basement. He
didn't let me read them, but I saw a postcard with a cross sketched
on it like a gravestone and the phrase "Wine of the sea, I die of
love." I felt exceedingly grown up because he let me sit with him
while he read, privy to his reflectively pursed lips. Another time he
was shaving, dressed only in his shorts. And when I touched his

back and told him how smooth it was, he laughed and told me women used to come for miles around to touch the skin of his back. I had seen photos of some of those women in an album—one fox-faced, posing with his hunting rifle, another with mysterious pale hair. I imagined the girls in long lines that snaked around the block, waiting to touch that smooth creamy skin.

He was bemused by his own wild past, but my sexual future seemed to worry him a lot. When I complained that I wasn't as pretty as my friend Sylvia, or that my nose was too big, he protested that I was beautiful. He would even call me out of my bedroom in my yellow silk nightie to show me off to company, but he was also clearly getting nervous. When I felt a tiny lump next to the nipple of one of my budding breasts, he rushed to phone the doctor. I sat on my bed in an agony of embarrassment while the doctor palpated the tender places. Afterwards, I heard him reassure my father that it was just normal development, not the breast cancer that had killed his mother.

It was the same with my period. (I was the first in my class to get it.) One day my father found a drop of blood on the toilet seat. "In all the years I've been married to your mother," he said, "I've never seen anything like this." Ladies didn't let gentlemen see what came out of their bodies. That was why, he said, examining my badly washed hands, he would never go out with a woman who had even a speck of dirt under her fingernails. Clearly here was an area where my mother's analytic thinking hadn't penetrated. My little brother, no doubt following my mother's advice, was allowed to finger himself under the table at dinner, and no one rebuked him. But my bleeding was something bad, like dirt or shit. My mother told me it was wonderful that I'd "become a woman," but she also stayed in bed during her periods, like a Victorian woman. My father, for his part, forbade me to horseback ride when I was menstruating for fear I'd scramble something inside. I rebelled and went anyway. Later, I gave a party, took my friends into my bedroom, announced that I had gotten my period and showed them, boys and girls alike, the drawer where I kept my pads. I wasn't going to stay in bed and be sick. I was going to flaunt it.

My father's double standard about sex (fine for him, worrisome for me) was linked in my mind with his views about class. The summer after seventh grade, some carpenters were working on our barn at the farm: a handsome black-haired man and his son and old father. I was restless and bored that summer—tired of reading endless horse stories—and I became something of a carpenter groupie.

One day I suggested inviting them to dinner. My father gently explained that every man had his place in the world. Otis, our hired man, was a good hunting companion, but much as one liked him, one wouldn't invite him for dinner. It was the same with the carpenters.

I was appalled. The idea of a man's "place" seemed to contradict my father's talk about equality. Also, my father had an air of camaraderie that I associated with people who worked with their hands. His stories of growing up in Newark added to this impression. He told me how he fought with the Irish street kids and ate black bread and molasses. How he worked his way up in the world until he made a million dollars. When I was small, I pictured him like the younger son in a fairy tale, braving ogres to get to the treasure. Somewhat later I saw him as Pip in *Great Expectations*.

My early impressions of my father's family were that the men were rough-and-ready fellows: Great-grandpa had marched on Georgia with General Sherman, and my father's father, David, ran a pony express. I pictured them with beards and sabers.

What I didn't understand was that while my mother's family were international bankers and as nearly aristocratic as Jews could be, my father's background was thoroughly middle class. His mother's Lutheran family operated a cigar store on Newark's main street, and when Grandpa David moved to Newark, he sold shoes retail. My father's first cousin Eddy told me later that my father's family felt he'd risen above them. "We didn't run in the same set he did," Eddy told me, "the Algonquin crowd, all that. But your father didn't care. He used to come over, shmooze, have dinner. I was just a little squirt, but he'd take me out for ice cream at Schrafft's."

Children are natural socialists. My father's refusal to invite the carpenters to dinner was my first hint that his liberal ideas went only so far. I knew the good things he did: helping downtrodden artists, raising money for Jewish immigrants, and working with the

Urban League against segregation. With childish logic I thought that caring for people also meant spending time with them.

Then there was the question of the communists who I knew believed in an exalted version of "sharing." Both my parents sympathized with communist views. But my father wouldn't take Alger Hiss's case because he was afraid it might hurt his family. Helen Buttenweiser, whose children also went to Dalton, not only took Alger's defense but kept his son Tony at her house for a year during the trial. I knew this because Alger's wife, Priscilla (Prue), taught English at Dalton and Tony was in my brother's class. Chris would come back with reports of a giant Shmoo named Nixon that Tony used as a punching bag. Even if it endangered his family, I wished my father would rush down on a white horse to save poor Prue from the reporters clustered like vultures around the school gates.

In a similar way, I had fantasies of my father loading the carpenters with gifts or at least offering them the use of our swimming pool. Since he insisted on a class barrier, I determined to break it. I flirted with them.

"Don't stand on your head that way in front of men," Mother told me. "Those baggy shorts show everything."

I see now that Mother was in the difficult position of many progressive parents. Having encouraged me to think of sex as good, it was hard to explain why it was also dangerous. Before she had gotten worried about the carpenters, Mother had assured me that making love was something to look forward to, telling me how you prepared by taking a long bath and rubbing oil on your body.

"Then when your husband comes in the door, you put your arms around each other. You'll see. It'll be very easy." But even though sex was good and even romantic and wonderful, it was apparently dangerous for little girls. Once, when I innocently sang, "She's broad where a broad should be broad," at dinner, Mother actually gave me a slap.

Her warnings only stimulated me. One day when it was very hot, I went so far as to lick a drop of sweat off the handsome carpenter's bare chest. At night, I lay on my bed—by then I had a room near the barn—fantasizing that he would pass by and see me in my yellow nightie.

One day I found myself alone, not with the handsome carpenter, but with his old father—whose nose was filled with alarming tufts of white hair. When he started to unbuckle his overalls, I asked him what he was doing, and he laughed and told me he had peed in his pants and had to change them. Then he came over and fondled my breasts through my T-shirt. "You're getting little titties," he said, "cute little titties," and he kissed me full on the lips. Mortified, I pulled myself away and ran out of the barn. I never told my mother. I didn't want to give her the satisfaction.

This was the last summer on the farm, the end point of an idyllic childhood. My father sold his half of the farm to Muriel in 1949. An old color photo shows me in a straw hat standing in a field of just-harvested wheat, hipless, no breasts to speak of, just on the edge of something new.

As several chinks appeared in my belief in parental infallibility, I turned more towards my friends and their culture. Until then, my father had been the arbiter of fashion for both me and my mother. I couldn't articulate my perception that Mother was split into an active artist self (including her sexually liberated side) and a submissive wife, but I began to be angry at her for accepting his dictation. I hated her boasting about her lack of contact with what she called "the world." Wasn't the world what you were supposed to find out about? I looked at her with pure loathing when in the midst of watering her plants, she'd break into Othello's lines about Desdemona: "She loved me for the dangers I had passed." I was going to encounter my own dangers. I was going to be glamorous *and* worldly wise.

Just about this time, I came up against my father's concept of ostentation. One day I came home from riding in Central Park and said I wanted a peacock blue riding outfit like Nancy Miller's. "It's garish," he said, "a sign of being nouveau." I stayed in my brown tweed jacket and unobtrusive jodhpurs.

Class meant knowing how to present yourself, being low-key, ladylike. In high school, I was friends with Phyllis Field, Marshall Field's elder daughter. Her luxurious apartment had two floors and a marble staircase. She had butlers in black and maids in white. I visited her once to share a physics lesson. When I got home I innocently asked my father why our apartment—it was eight rooms, including a maid's room and three baths—was so much smaller than Phyllis's. We weren't as rich as they were, he explained, frowning, but the Fields invited me to be with their daughter because our family had class.

Later, I puzzled about his reaction. I liked Phyllis's apartment with its marbles and silk-canopied beds, but did my father like it? It was the sort of thing he usually called "ostentatious." Then why was he proud that they had invited me? Was it because my family was Jewish that we had to be particularly careful about showing off, since that was supposedly a Jewish characteristic?

One time, when I was still in eighth grade, I got my hair cut and set without asking Daddy's advice. I ran home happily shaking my fabulous new curls.

"You look like a secretary," my father said, making my cheeks burn with a combination of shame and anger.

When I gave my first dancing party, my friend Sylvia arrived in a low-cut green dress. Sylvia had been my rival since fourth grade, when she captivated the boys with her black braids and long-lashed blue-green eyes. My father stared at her wonderfully white skin and the voluptuous swell of her breasts. "Definitely whorish," he muttered after a minute.

After that, whorish was what I wanted to be. I started using swear words like "bitch" and "bastard" and slang like "yaa" and "shadup," words my father hated as much as he did tight sweaters and rouge. I gravitated towards the faster girls, resisting his attempts to keep me in little-girl clothes.

I also began to think about my father's past and realized in brief bursts of consciousness that he had one standard for me and another for the rest of the world. I found a copy of *God's Little Acre* in the living room, with pages at the back summarizing the obscenity trial and giving my father's name as counsel. So I knew, as I read about bizarre couplings in the red clay fields of Georgia, that my father defended this book. I listed the title as my favorite book on the book page in my diary, next to a peer-recommended tale of gang rape and violence, *The Amboy Dukes*. But I couldn't quite figure out what my father was defending. Was it the right of albinos to screw young girls? Or was it just the right to make up stories about it?

Another book I found on my parents' shelves was *The Kinsey Report,* which claimed to reveal not what people imagined, but what they did. Since Dalton was so permissive, they didn't object to my writing a book report on it for school. I was impressed by the facts about masturbation, oral sex, adultery, and cohabitation with farm animals. Kinsey's attitude was nonjudgmental. What I didn't know at the time was that *The Kinsey Report* marked the start of a new era of matter-of-factness in the sexual revolution. He wasn't interested in moral questions of good or bad, he simply observed what people were doing.

Ironically, some of Kinsey's most vehement opponents were psychoanalysts. They were a bit in the same position as progressive parents. They had let the cat out of the bag, and now it was off and running out of control. Not only did Kinsey disagree with some of Freud's most cherished notions, like sublimation, but he separated sex and love. He thought that what people did was normal, regardless of its psychological causes. Even analysts who felt that Kinsey had exposed the hypocrisy of civilized morality were upset by this "zoological" approach.

Though I thought about sex a lot, my experience in eighth grade was mostly limited to fantasy. My father had fostered several children through Save the Children, and I took to writing one of them, Henri, because of the passionate way he signed his letters: *Je t'embrasse, avec milles bisous.* I would lie in bed repeating *Je t'embrasse,* thinking not of Henri, who was ugly and had jug ears, but of Jonas, a handsome blond boy in my class.

The first time a boy asked me for a real date was February 11, 1950. I dwelt on it at length in my diary. My thirteen-year-old prose was operatic: there was a party with whirling couples, a jealous rival. Adjectives abound, my preferred one being "marvelous," but I couldn't describe sensations yet. My prose style favored action. This is my description of the fateful moment after Jonas invited me to the movies:

"Have I ever kissed you?" he asked, pulling me into a corner.

"No," I said.

"Would you like to make this a first time?"

"Sure."

It seemed obligatory after letting our lips touch to declare myself in love. "I can't help it," I wrote, following the script of romance. "I'm falling in love."

The date itself was more problematic. Up until then, I confessed to my diary, I had thought necking and petting were "disgusting." But while watching *The Hasty Heart* with Jonas in the dark Orpheum Theatre, I had a revelation. "I loved every minute and I'm not ashamed," I wrote. "He is the perfect lover."

But though I talked big, I was still very much a child. There are smudges in the book where I erased the most graphic details—the way Jonas had taken my hand and pushed it down on his erection. I had known this boy most of my life. The tiny appendage that I had examined with interest in kindergarten had swollen to enormous proportions. It was rock hard and thrusting into my hand only a zipper away.

When I got home, I took my teddy bear, a large golden-brown bear with velvet pads and only one eye, and gave him a ferocious whipping with my belt. Every stroke I gave him made me cry harder. "Damn it," I cried, "damn." In that moment, I felt as if I'd lived my whole life, done everything, and there was nothing left to experience.

I didn't go out with Jonas again. I even criticized his disgusting jokes. "He doesn't know how to handle himself," I confided to my diary.

My father's first heart attack was like a bomb exploding in the middle of our family. Everything that had been secure was threatened, and much of the energy I'd put into growing up was deflected into worry. At first I couldn't grasp it, couldn't believe that my strong-as-a-rock father was actually sick. Hadn't he boasted of his health, boasted that he'd never had even a toothache? But there it was. He'd gone out on a spring morning to play baseball with my eight-year-old brother and come staggering back through the front door clutching his chest.

A few weeks after his heart attack, I was at Dalton dissecting a frog in our freshman science class. It had been anesthetized but was still alive and its tiny heart was still beating, pulsing out its froggy blood. Suddenly I saw my father under his ballooning oxygen tent struggling to breathe, and my own heart began to thump and lurch in an alarming manner. From that time on, I had no control over it;

if I even heard the word "heart," my own would buck and plunge like a frightened horse.

Once I was sitting on his lap and noticed some flakes of dandruff on the shoulder of his pajamas. "You'd have dandruff too if you'd been lying in bed for such a long time," he said crankily when I told him. "The damn nurse should have massaged my scalp." Mortified, I threw my arms around his neck and burst into tears.

His illness seemed to make him worry more about me. He became fussier about my manners and behavior. One night when we were all at dinner and I was dreamily pushing peas onto my knife and tipping them into my mouth, my father suddenly slapped the knife out of my hand.

"No daughter of mine will eat peas off a knife," he said. "You hear me." I ran to my room, crying. He had never hit me before.

My father's worst fear was that I'd lose my virginity and not be able to make a successful marriage. I had started to go to necking parties and was experimenting with makeup. I have a long account in my diary of a double date in which we were driven around New York for hours by one boy's chauffeur while we searched the city for something exciting to do. We tried unsuccessfully to get into a movie called *Illicit Love* and ended up, four rich, bored children, wrestling on someone's couch with the lights off. On this occasion, I got my first real kiss. I had no idea that lips, the same lips I used for eating and drinking, could suddenly fill my awareness. I clung to the boy. He seemed surprised. I was too hot for a good girl—though I wasn't doing anything more than kissing.

In the middle of freshman year, my father brought home Ed, a boy whose father worked in my father's law office. Perhaps he thought this was a boy he could control. Ed's looks recommended him right away—chiseled nose, blue eyes, well-muscled body. He had a portfolio of drawings to show Mother. "My teacher says I have the technique down," he said, "but I could use some pointers on style. And you seem just the lady to give them to me." I was impressed. Not only was he a senior, but he worked with nude models. It seemed the height of sophistication. My mother, on the other hand, riffled through his charcoal sketches of naked women with her eyebrows raised. "A bit like Norman Rockwell," she said finally. I blushed, embarrassed, but Ed thought it was a compliment.

"Dad brought home a dreamboat," I wrote in my diary, "and we're going to the movies next week." My father breathed a sigh of relief when we started to go out regularly. His girl would be watched over even if he weren't there.

When Judy Johnson saw me and Ed dancing cheek to cheek at a school dance, she said we should be thinking about art, not boys. Just to show her a girl could have both, I increased my own literary efforts.

When my father was so sick, I wrote my first passably good story, about a boy whose mother feels triumphant when her son's colt dies—she'd been jealous of the attention the boy gave him. It was a grim little tale, but somehow writing it made me feel much better.

Judy read the story. Whereas her own talent was epic and impersonal, she said, mine was clearly tied up with my family. She pronounced with dazzling assurance that I was to be D. H. Lawrence to her Malory.

It shouldn't be surprising that Judy saw us both as male artists. There weren't many women to use as role models in the early 1950s. In high school Dalton became an all-girl school, so girls had to play the male parts in theater productions. I was Sir Walter Raleigh in *Elizabeth and Essex*. I wanted to be the queen, but I'd been Rosalind in *As You Like It* the year before, wearing in satisfying alternation a masculine doublet and a wedding dress covered with imitation pearls.

My father died in August 1951 at a hospital in Maine where he had been vacationing with my mother. He was fifty-one. While he was dying, I was riding in the Camp Kinya horse show in Vermont. I wanted to win a ribbon to give him, to encourage him to get well. My horse was called Retreat. I had ridden my heart out—Retreat was a loser by nature but I raked his sides with my spurs, and sheer will got us over the jumps. My whole being was concentrated on keeping my form, hands on his neck, eyes right between his ears, while preventing the wretched horse from balking. It was a moment of pure joy when the riding counselor pinned a blue ribbon to Retreat's bridle.

And then, while I was still hot with triumph, the same counselor called me outside and told me, flatly, that my father was dead. I blinked, too shocked to cry.

They brought me my ribbons in the camp infirmary where I was resting on an iron cot, shivering despite the August heat. I started going over my conversations with Mother. "It's all right. He's out of the woods," she'd said in her last call. So I had every reason to relax and trust. Her voice was faint because of the bad connection, but it was sure. And he'd told me he'd be all right himself, that he was going to beat this thing. He'd written me humorous letters about how "little Mums" was tootling around the lake leaving him wrapped up in a blanket on a deck chair. He even sent me a stick drawing of himself getting thin and healthy.

I flew back on a plane with a woman I didn't know, who had arrived to accompany me. I sat staring out the window at the clouds, fat and fluffy as giant sheep, and tried to lose myself in all that whiteness. Then through a gap in the clouds I saw the ground, coming at me, and imagined the plane shooting out of control. As I listened, the motor seemed to falter. I could see the plane wing out my window and I imagined it dipping, carrying me down in a slow spiral.

When I got to the apartment, I went down the long hall to my mother. I don't know what I expected. She was in bed propped up against some white pillows looking dazed and haggard. I felt awkward. I so much wanted her to put her arms around me and tell me we'd be all right—but clearly she couldn't. I thrust my ribbons at her and for a moment it seemed there was a flicker of interest in her eyes, then she put them gently away, her eyes dulling as though a curtain had been pulled across them.

Muriel Gardiner stood next to me—she had flown to Maine to bring Mother home—and I felt her arm around my shoulder. After a few more minutes, when Mother tried to rally herself and talk to me, Muriel gently pushed me toward the door. I sat at the dining room table and looked at my father's obituary in the *Times*.

I noticed the writer had made a small mistake and I wanted to show Mother.

"No. Don't," Muriel said. "You must be very careful with your mother. She's close to a nervous breakdown."

I looked at her, not understanding. Cars break down. But mothers are supposed to stay the same. Mine had always been nervous and demanding. I was used to that by now. But I thought I could take care of her. I pictured myself bringing her endless cups of tea. We were still a family, weren't we? My brother, my mother, and I. We'd manage.

Chapter

5

*She was like a forest, like the dark interlacing of
the oak-wood, humming inaudibly with myriad
unfolding buds. Meanwhile the birds of desire
were asleep in the vast interlaced intricacy of her
body.* —D. H. LAWRENCE

fter the cremation, Mother seemed calmer. I had no idea of the
seriousness of her condition. But Muriel, fearing a breakdown,
arranged for a trained nurse to sit by her bed every night and for a
new psychoanalyst, Marianne Kris, to take her on as a patient.
Muriel and Marianne had attended the legendary Wednesday meetings together in Vienna, along with a core group of the early analysts including Anna Freud and Helene Deutsch.

Marianne's father was Oscar Rie, pediatrician to Freud's children. Marianne worked at the Child Development Clinic at Yale.
Her husband, Ernst, was one of the leading investigators of the psychology of art. They were highly cultivated, and the match between
Mother and Marianne was a happy one, broken only by the analyst's death. Though I question the morality of keeping a patient in
treatment for thirty years, I'm convinced that Kris came to love my
mother if not to cure her.

On her first visit to Dr. Kris, Mother took off her wedding ring
and hurled it across the room. "Don't, Ethel," Kris said softly.
Mother always remembered that compassionate use of her first
name: strict Freudian analysts in those days were formal. They
could see you for twenty years and still call you Mrs. or Miss. Just
as they could sit for days saying nothing but "I see," or "How do
you feel about that?" In any case Mother was cheered by hearing
her name. It seemed to signify that Kris would care for her in a special way, and Mother never stopped trying to get more of it.

Taking off the ring so angrily, Kris told her, would have meant denying her love, all the years of her marriage. Mother went across the room, picked up the ring and put it back on.

The ring stayed on, but everything else started to change. She dropped her best friend, the wife of our family doctor, who had refused to fly to Maine to care for my father. Other friends were shed because they didn't fit the new life she envisioned as a woman without a husband. She was bored by most of my father's client-friends and other lawyers. She kept only the friends who had a vital connection to art, like my father's partner Jimmy Grossman and his wife, who moved in literary circles and were close friends of Diana and Lionel Trilling. Her other friends were women with whom she had strong emotional ties, like Muriel Gardiner or Miggie Beller, an old Princeton friend who had been engaged to my father and had with great tact managed to continue being friends with the couple. Mother never showed any jealousy of her.

The jettisoning of friends was part of a general reorganization. I watched as, during the next months, Mother stripped down our apartment. The bourgeois decor that marked her life with my father disappeared: the dark blue drapes in the dining room, the wallpaper with gold fleur-de-lis, the oval portraits of my father's parents, all went. The dining room was done in an off-white that would show paintings to the greatest advantage and she hung it with her and Gorky's work.

The living room got the same treatment. There had been big deep sofas and armchairs arranged around a central fireplace. But now there was only a small, uncomfortable sitting area made up of Grandma's ornately carved sofa and matching chairs.

The rest of the room, stripped of its rugs, became Mother's studio. It would have been hard not to conclude that my father's death released her to be herself. Paradoxically, the furniture she kept was all from her childhood home.

My father's leaving her with teenage me must have seemed like a replay of her own father's death when she was just a few years older than I. She had comforted her widowed mother, often sleeping in her bed. But though I tried to comfort my mother, I rarely succeeded. And occupied as she was by her pain, I could hardly expect her to help me with mine.

Despite the fact that she saw Dr. Kris every weekday and relied on her as a powerful maternal figure, Mother was catapulted back into the time of past abandonments: her father's death, Dr. Gluck's desertion. Dr. Kris urged her to paint her grief and rage. A few weeks after my father died, she set up a fresh canvas on her easel. Her painting had always been associated in my mind with the farm, lush green leaves and cows grazing. I was hopeful. I told myself that our family was like a tree with a limb cut off; the cut would heal and we would go on.

But these new paintings and the ones that followed were entirely different from the idyllic pastorals of life on the farm. Instead of bulls and peacocks, there were violent gashes of paint in red and white and black. What shocked me, though I couldn't recognize it then, was the anger that she expressed in her art. She wasn't just sad, grieving the way I was—she was furious. The colors were like blows. A little later, she started working with glass, shattering it and gluing the sharp fragments onto pieces of wood to make collages. She played Gluck's *Orpheus* at top volume and sang along with it in a desperate voice, "*Che faro senza Eurydice?*" Orpheus's lament for his dead wife still strikes a chill in me.

While Mother dropped her friends, changed the furniture, and started to paint again, I thought about my father, determined to be loyal to his memory. "Ed is so sweet," I wrote in my diary—I still saw him steadily—"but I should remember Daddy, not think of Ed. I must make something of myself, must become somebody."

Mother had given me my father's college diary from Princeton and I devoured it. Comparing myself with him as a college student in 1918, I found myself lacking. He thought about world affairs and I didn't. He'd even enlisted to fight for his country, though the war ended before he got to the front. Searching through old albums, I found photos of him in his army uniform, tight puttees, a broad-brimmed felt hat, jodhpurlike trousers. His eyes and the determined tilt of his chin showed the same puritanical young man who wrote in his diary that he was disgusted by sex.

Further on in the album, though, there were snapshots of him in a bathing suit clowning with a young Harpo Marx. My father at thirty was clearly a liberated man. He was laughing, surrounded by sophisticated young women in bathing suits, smoking and drinking. I put all these photographs in an envelope in my drawer, knowing by now that he didn't want me to follow this example. He wanted me to take on sterner virtues.

I was sorry I'd curled my hair and given him back talk. I washed the makeup off my face and cut my hair in the severe style he liked. I'd work hard and try to succeed. People would look at me and say, "She really has what it takes. Just like her dad."

When I wasn't reading my father's diary or writing poems, I hung around the kitchen with Weasal, the immense black lady who cooked for us, eating cookies. Weasal (short for Louise), made me what she called "feel-good" dishes. One in particular, a mixture of mashed potatoes, tomatoes, and crumbled bacon, I called mush and found perfectly comforting. Mother only cooked on Weasal's day off and acted as if grilling a lamb chop was incredibly burdensome. Needless to say, I never learned to cook. Before I got married, Weasal would give me a crash course on how to broil a hamburger.

The last important thing my father had done for me was to bring me Ed. Nothing could fill the emptiness, but it helped. When Ed's father died ten days after my father died, it seemed providential. Our fathers had been friends. We were both bereft.

Still, when Ed asked me to go steady, I wasn't sure. I was only fifteen, after all, Ed just seventeen. And I often saw boys I found more attractive. When I asked Mother what to do, she promptly turned to Dr. Kris. Nothing important was done without asking the analyst's opinion. When I think of my mother at that time, I see an image of Kris with her large gray eyes looking calmly over my mother's shoulder.

"She thinks it's good for you to try having a committed relationship," Mother relayed back to me. Kris's endorsement was probably only meant to give me freedom to experiment, but I felt nudged.

Besides the doctor's opinion, I had the message from my hero D. H. Lawrence: my woman's task was to respond to the mysterious blood forces. Mother gave me a complete set of his works for my birthday and I read them transfixed. The combination of sex and mystical pronouncements was irresistible.

It was an interesting present from mother to daughter. For one thing, Lawrence was at the center of the most celebrated obscenity trial of the century for his depiction of Lady Chatterley's affair with her gamekeeper. Lawrence's intensely poetic—and erotic—descriptions of lovemaking became my model of how things should be between men and women. Mother had always said sex was beautiful and her gift seemed to give me a green light.

Lawrence was both deeply concerned with sex—he thought Freud was right about its importance—and deeply conservative about women. At the time, I didn't mind the fact that Lawrence believed women shouldn't think, but simply exist and soothe men with the richness of their presence. It was a deep substratum of the culture that I took for granted. But I did notice the power men seemed to have over women and the way male sexual energy somehow forced women to give up their independent wills, and submit. Though I would have been horrified at the time to think that my mother had sexual fantasies similar to mine, she obviously did. Her early paintings were full of Lawrentian images of sexualized flowers, such as giant white lilies, set next to flamboyantly masculine red or black bulls: Beauty and Power. Reviewers noticed that many of the "radiant poetic pastels" in her first successful show at the Passedoit Gallery had titles drawn from Lawrence's work and suggested the "forces of nature in a brilliant shimmer of color and sweeping line." Mother said more clearly that she was painting "the poetry of sex."

Giving me the books was in part a way of passing on an essentially romantic attitude. Unconsciously, I would do the same with my eldest daughter, giving her my dog-eared copies of Lawrence when she was a teenager. She was outraged. "How can you like stuff like this?" she asked me. "This ridiculous worship of the penis. He hates women's bodies. There isn't a description of a breast anywhere. Look at this," and she read me a long passage about bulbous phallic lilies. "Besides, he's a homosexual," she said and slammed the book shut.

As a parent, Mother seems to have been only slightly more permissive than my father. But as an artist, her central premise was passion. My father had left his pubescent daughter with a boy whom he thought was safe, but Mother's romanticism and Dr. Kris's approval were pushing me toward sexual exploration. Meanwhile, I had decided that I was going to be an artist too. When my schoolmates made me class poet, I took it as a sign of vocation.

I made every effort to force my situation with Ed into a "Lawrentian" mold. When we went down to Miggie Beller's place in Princeton for a weekend, I tried hard to act like one of Lawrence's women, sitting in Ed's bedroom immobile and silent, trying to be mysterious, until finally he carried me over to his bed and started to kiss me. Once there, I spread my hair behind me on the pillow like the doomed heroine I'd seen in a vampire movie. He cried and told me how much he loved me.

"I thought you'd never want me," he confessed between kisses. "You were my goddess."

"You mean you thought I was a snob," I said.

He laughed. "Well, your mother sure is. You said she was horrified that my grandma spoke Yiddish. She acted as if it was a disease."

"Well, I like it," I told him. What I didn't tell him was that it seemed deliciously lower class. Ed wasn't a gamekeeper, but he was just foreign enough. We didn't make love, but we kissed until our lips were sore.

On weekends Ed and I often went with Mother to Dr. Kris's place in Connecticut—by now Mother was totally dependent, and saw Kris on Saturdays as well as during the week. Going to an analyst's country home for an appointment would be unheard of today with the insistence on clear boundaries, and I don't know whether Kris did it with anyone else. In any case, Mother was always particularly tense before—and after—her sessions. Her voice on the drive out would be high with an edge of hysteria: she would toss her beautiful head, bite her lip, or roll her eyes, conversing with herself about the cruelty of her fate. She drove us at dangerously high speeds, and I'd be so tense by the time we arrived that Ed's caresses, as we lay by Dr. Kris's lake, were not only exciting but provided much-needed soothing. Sometimes we couldn't wait and started necking in the backseat of the car. But I remained a virgin.

After one of these trips, I wrote a poem called "Rebellion" about Ed standing naked on a dam, water drops covering him like jewels. It concluded, "To hell with the mores of a scornful world, the frigid virgins afraid of love." I submitted it to the Dalton literary magazine, where it created quite a sensation.

My mother, with Dr. Kris's advice, supported my attempt at poetry. She simply suggested I cut the florid lines about "crimson waves of desire" and "soul-searing shame." She seemed unconcerned with anything but the artistic value of my work. Though, who knows, maybe when she was saying, "It's a lovely poem, darling," she was actually worrying about what the teachers would think. Still, if I was trying to get a rise out of her, I hadn't succeeded.

After a while Mother must have confessed that she was risking all our lives on the Connecticut roads, because Kris suggested she get a driver. Bill was blond and handsome. While driving us, he often looked into his mirror and observed Ed's and my goings-on in the backseat. In an old snapshot, I am in a tight sweater looking bemused while Bill and Ed tie me to a tree.

Bill fit my Lawrentian model even better than Ed, which Mother didn't like at all. "He's not a plaything for you," she told me. "He's there for me. Besides, he's a married man and his wife's expecting a baby."

"Everyone's there for you," I muttered under my breath.

She lifted her hand to slap me, but I ran out of the room.

One day I let Bill help me with my Latin in the kitchen. Mother came in and found him in his shirtsleeves, no coat, arm around me. "What do you think you're doing?" she asked me after she'd motioned him to the other room.

"Homework," I said.

"Well, stop it," she told me, "and stop smirking at me; I hate it."

"It's just my face," I screamed at her in an unusual display of anger. "Leave me alone."

Just before Christmas, I was lying on the floor in our darkened dining room watching television with Eddie, and he put his hand under my sweater. My breast didn't completely fill the cup of my bra, which mortified me. But when he finally reached my skin and firmly cupped my breast, I forgot all about my diminutive size and gasped with pleasure.

How good it felt to have him lie on top of me for the first time, how he trembled all over, how his manhood—I always thought of it in Lawrentian terms—pressed on me down there, making a melting pleasure radiate out along my limbs.

It was about this time that I asked Mother how far I should go with Eddie. She talked it over with Kris and they decided I should have a psychiatrist of my own to talk these questions over with. At a time when she was barely able to keep going herself, Mother felt overwhelmed by the responsibility of raising an adolescent. She worried that she'd tell me the wrong thing. It was much less anxiety-producing to let someone else make the vital decisions.

The analytic community had grown during the 1930s and 1940s with an influx of refugees from Nazi Europe, among them Heinz Hartman, Rudolph Loewenstein, the Krises, Berta Bornstein, Gustav Bychowski. Lawrence Kubie, a wealthy analyst friend of ours, helped many of the immigrants set up new homes and practices. Most of them, like Drs. Kris and Eissler, lived on Central Park West. Some, like Gustav Bychowski, lived on the Upper East Side. The places they lived coincided with the boundaries of my childhood world, whereas most of the artists lived in the Village.

Yet there was a strong connection between analysts and artists. The artists went into analysis for relief of their problems—and many wrote novels or scripts using Freudian themes—while the analysts probed the mysteries of the creative process. Kubie wrote a book on genius and analyzed Moss Hart, George S. Kaufman's collaborator. Eissler, also obsessed with genius, wrote on Goethe and Hamlet. Gregory Zilboorg analyzed Elia Kazan, father of a Dalton friend. Marianne Kris analyzed Marilyn Monroe. Even Mother's interminable analysis was written about for the *Psychoanalytic Quarterly* by a literary critic, Jeffrey Berman, who felt that despite the thirty-year sequel with Kris, Deutsch's earlier work with Mother was a great success.

I knew many of the analysts through their children. One of my best friends was Bychowski's daughter Monica, an intense black-eyed girl who arrived at Dalton from Poland during the war. She told us how her father, not believing in the danger, practically had to be dragged out of Poland at the last minute by her mother. They lost everything—their beautiful house, his art collection, books. I spent a great deal of time at their Fifth Avenue apartment overlooking Central Park, and through Monica met her best friend, Lizzie Loewenstein, analyst Rudolph Lowenstein's daughter. When I was a freshman in high school, I dated Heinz Hartmann's son Ernest, who took me to *Kiss Me, Kate* and then tried to kiss me, fleeing in panic after we bumped noses. He was terribly Germanic, clicking his heels and bowing over my hand, and even then clearly an intellectual. I only saw Tony Kris, Dr. Kris's son, once, but I thought he was dreamy and was dying to go out with him.

I wasn't aware when I visited their children that Loewenstein, Hartmann and Kris were responsible for an important new development in psychoanalysis, ego psychology, which emphasized the ego's ability to master reality. There was a shift away from earlier ideas of freeing the instincts. Given what had just happened in Nazi Germany, perhaps too much permissiveness was dangerous. By that time, failures were also being reported in the area of permissive child rearing. It appeared that permitting expression of violent hostility, such as death wishes against a sibling, vastly increased a child's insecurity. The conclusion of many analysts, including Anna Freud, was that people needed some protection against the force of their drives.

It's one of the ironies of my situation that the famous child analyst whom Muriel Gardiner suggested for me, Berta Bornstein, acted as if she had never heard of ego mastery and continually encouraged me to express my sexuality. Bornstein was Muriel's closest friend among the analysts. It was she who had warned Muriel to get out of Vienna after the Anschluss, and Muriel referred to her affectionately as Bertele. However, Bornstein had seen Connie as a very young child—Muriel was worrying about raising her without a father—and Connie hadn't liked her.

Berta Bornstein was certainly one of the scariest-looking people I'd ever seen. She was short and dumpy with wispy gray hair and a red birthmark covering a large part of one side of her face. Besides this, she had a nervous mannerism of putting a cold glass or something else to her forehead as though she were suffering from terrible headaches.

In the first sessions, Bornstein made me lie down on her couch and free-associate. All I could think of was how ugly her birthmark was and whether her husband, if she had one, could possibly sleep with her. When I wasn't thinking that, I would compulsively imagine sucking a penis. I would have died rather than tell her either of these thoughts, so eventually she let me sit up, and asked me about my masturbation fantasies. "Don't worry," she told me, when I said

I'd never masturbated, "you did it just like everyone else. Only you feel too guilty to admit it." When I told her about riding bareback, she almost jumped out of her seat. "But of course that's how you got gratification," she said. Eventually she confined herself to giving me practical advice. She wanted to have me fitted with a diaphragm, but she was afraid that if she did I'd tell everyone at school. Certainly her talk about masturbation and encouragement to get a diaphragm only confused me. Though I clearly needed attention and nurturing more than sex, I also needed to develop some independence. The fact that my sexuality was being managed by my shrink only made me feel more like a baby.

Bornstein might profitably have asked me how I felt having a mother who, though she spoke brilliantly about literature, couldn't talk to me about my feelings and had to dump me on a stranger. If my father had lived, we would certainly have fought over sex, but not only was my mother in such fragile shape, she was also so damned sympathetic. I couldn't get any distance, not to speak of mounting a rebellion.

This may not be fair. Perhaps Bornstein saw that I was going to "do it" and simply wanted to make sure that at least I didn't get pregnant. Or maybe she didn't want me getting married just so I could have sex. She was quite scornful of Ed, saying, at one point, "You're not really thinking of marrying that little bourgeois, are you?"

Initially, Mother may have thought Bornstein would help control me, while she, Mother, remained my confidante. Muriel was enlisted to help too. Mother asked her to keep an eye on us when we visited the farm. Of course we spent our time kissing. Once, holed up in my old nursery, Ed was emboldened to strip. It was my first experience of feeling his naked body. I was shocked and frightened by all the hair: he was covered with fur. At first, it was all I could do to lie next to him. At about one in the morning, having fallen asleep, I heard Muriel at the window.

"It's very late," she said—I heard her muffled laugh—"and I promised your mother I'd see that you behaved."

Though I certainly wasn't ready to settle down at fifteen, sexual exploration had a momentum of its own. My memories are round and bright, full of sensations.

Eddie had a pair of cream-colored slacks, and I was riveted to the way the fabric draped over his erection, the way it rose, the exact degree it stood out from his body. I began to think of it as a little homunculus with a personality of its own. We named it Melvin and I have a photo of Ed in a tight bathing suit, with "love from Melvin and Ed" written in his best calligraphy at the bottom. The beauty of my flirtation with Melvin was that it was unconsummated: the partial knowing, the gradual disrobing, was delicious.

I remember one late afternoon in the backseat of the car. Bill was driving me and Ed and Mother back from Dr. Kris's country place. Under cover of a lap robe I was stroking Eddie's stomach as we sped along, and he suddenly sucked in his breath, letting me slip my hand beneath his belt. So this is really it, I marveled, feeling Melvin's heat.

Another time, at a beach outing with Mom and Chris, after we'd kissed for hours in the water, Ed lingered in the dressing room. I went back to see what was keeping him.

"It got frozen stiff," he whispered through a crack in the gray boards. "I can't get it down." He'd been trying to jerk off.

Through a knothole, I could see him move his hand with its silver ID bracelet confidently up and down. I was fascinated by his casual mastery of his sexual organ. I wasn't even sure what mine consisted of (or where they were). Every morning at school my friends Monica and Sylvia sat in the hall and swapped information. When I told them that Ed and I couldn't find my clitoris, that it mainly hurt down there, Monica looked at me quizzically. "Gosh. I found mine at six, climbing trees," she said. "Maybe you should read *Ideal Marriage*; it has illustrations."

"Forget about it," Sylvia advised, "just play with his dick."

"She knows you like ze penis," Bornstein said when I related this conversation to her. "That's good. Very unneurotic." From a Freudian viewpoint it meant I was moving toward the genital sex that was considered the sign of maturity. But from the beginning of my relations with Ed, it was the idea of sex that interested me more than doing it. I liked talking about it, trying it out as fiction. Anybody but my analyst would have seen I wasn't ready for the real thing.

Chapter

6

The suicidal person leaves his psychological skeleton in the survivor's closet.
                              —EDWIN SHNEIDMAN

*E*d joined the Navy in 1952, when the war in Korea was winding down, and went off to boot camp at the Great Lakes. It was eleventh grade. Mother and I were women alone: our men dead or off bayoneting dummies. It made me try again for contact. One day when she was studying the Gorky paintings stacked against the living room wall—she was turning the catalogue she'd written for the Whitney into a book—I came up behind her and told her I wanted to be an artist too, a poet.

"Art is always there when you need it," she said. "It doesn't leave you in the lurch. Poor Gorky," she added, without turning around. "Such a great artist and such a tragic life." She crouched down and resumed her scrutiny of the painting.

She bought me a copybook for my poems, filled with green unlined paper, and sat in bed reading my phrases aloud, beating with her fingers on the covers: "'Under such beauty lies my heart'; hmmm, the image is lovely, but the rhythm? And you've misspelled 'brilliant,' darling." Neither of us mentioned that I was writing about my father's flower covered grave. Still, sharing images with her gave me an uncanny sense of common ground. The poems I wrote about my sadness were the closest I ever came to talking with her about my father's death.

She also read my poems about Ed, scanning my feelings with an inscrutable air. We didn't discuss those feelings, of course. We talked about style. "This has a Greek simplicity," she would say, when she read lines about my being so unhappy I couldn't find words to express it. "It's very pure."

I don't know if I sensed a crisis coming, but she was suddenly more anxious, cried more, got unpredictably angry. To steady her, I wrote a poem invoking her love for my father. The images were from the Twenty-Third Psalm, the one read at my father's memorial, and depicted my mother at the edge of a cliff contemplating suicide.

> Stop yet a moment to remember
> When the wheat fields were golden
> And your heart sang with love
> Have the courage to remember
> Though so tempted to forget.

I attributed her worsening moods to my father's death, but later I realized that her desperation that winter was over her Gorky book. I didn't understand how much the book meant to her or how she had imaginatively fused her life with Gorky's. In her later journal, she writes about a portrait she planned to do of herself with Gorky. She eventually left herself out, but in her mind she was there with him. A sort of twin.

Like Mother, Gorky had an early phase of marital happiness during which he produced radiant work—steeped like her own in the poetry of sex. Like her, Gorky suffered the loss of his loved one, and painted anguished canvases with names like *Agony* and *Charred Beloved*. She must have thought of following his example and killing herself when my father died. But she fought it by becoming Gorky's champion. In bringing his work to the public, she was saving herself. When she wrote the catalogue for the Whitney memorial in 1951, Lloyd Goodrich, the director of the museum, asked her to trim it. She did so with a great deal of pain. Mother hated criticism.

Much worse was Goodrich's rejection of her completed Gorky book. Now she was devastated.

One morning, a few days after I gave Mother my poem about courage, I was sitting in my room reading when Weasal came in and asked me if I'd go see about her. "Your mother's usually up around six and it's past ten. Maybe she's not feeling well. Why don't you just take a look?" "Why don't you," I answered, burrowing down in my chair, knowing perfectly well that Weasal wouldn't take a liberty like that. Then I looked hard at her and saw she was really worried. She stood there shifting from one foot to another, her enormous weight of flesh straining the fabric of her uniform. "Okay," I said.

The scene takes place in a perpetually present tense. It is the moment when my mother became someone else, familiar but strangely alien. I walk down the hall and open the door of her bedroom a crack and look in. She is lying in her bed with her head turned the other way. I can hear her snoring lightly. I tiptoe around the side of the bed expecting her to startle and jump up, ask me why I'm disturbing her. Can't I see she needs to sleep? But she doesn't move. Her mouth is slightly open and I can see the veins just under the skin. I touch her arm gently. "Mom?" She doesn't respond.

I take her arm, just below the strap of her peach silk nightgown; my fingers sink into the soft skin. I start to shake her, first softly then harder. "Mom," I say. "Mom, wake up, Mom." Her head flops back and forth, but she doesn't open her eyes. For a moment more, I stare at the little violet veins in the lids, then I see an empty bottle of sleeping pills on the floor. I run back to the kitchen and tell Weasal to call an ambulance.

After that the whole rescue scene unrolls like a film in slow motion. I was watching, but somehow I was disassociated from the men in helmets and black rubber boots who came through the front door, one of them incongruously holding an ax, and rushed down the hall to the bedroom. A few minutes later they came out with Mother strapped to a stretcher.

I had been one girl when I went into the room and another by the time the firemen came to take my mother to the hospital. What she had done made a breach of trust between us that never healed.

We had become a family that was dependent on outside support. In her iron lung Mother exemplified it perfectly. Chris and I were doing only slightly better. No one had to breathe for us, but we were still too young to manage. Our guardians were our therapists. Bornstein and Kris conferred and then Bornstein talked with my father's brother, Uncle Herman, and Weasal. I imagine it was Bornstein who felt it would be too traumatic for us to visit Mother in the hospital. Or perhaps it was Uncle Herman, who tried to reassure Mother—she later told me, unhappily—that we were fine without her.

But of course we weren't fine. Ellen, the daughter of a friend, was in an iron lung unable to move as a result of polio. She turned the pages of her book with a gadget she activated by blinking her eyelashes. I thought about Ellen and I thought about my mother in a round tube of iron having the breath pumped into her. But I couldn't feel anything except fear.

One of the worst parts for a self-conscious adolescent was how an attempted suicide looked to other people. Herman was clearly outraged and most other people didn't know how to react. When the firemen took her out the front door, I was already worrying what the elevator men would think.

Mother came home from the hospital with two trained nurses watching her in shifts morning and night and, soon after, someone came and put bars on the windows. She hated being guarded by the nurses and was sure Chris and I were plotting with them against her. Every day she went in a taxi with one of the nurses to Dr. Kris. Her therapy didn't relieve what went on at home. I lived in a kind of limbo where it seemed rude to comment when the smiling mother vanished into a nasty one. I could never ask, "Why did you do that, why did you slap me? Why did you call me bitch? You don't look like yourself. You look as though you hate me."

Just once, when we had a terrible argument in which she screamed and got hysterical, I remember her apologizing, or making an attempt. She'd lost control, she said, because of something that was going on in her analysis. Dr. Kris had explained it to her. It wasn't really me she was so angry at. But what good did that do me?

What I wanted was for her to sit down with me and say, "That must have hurt you a lot when I tried to kill myself. You must have felt I didn't love you but . . ."

But there never has been a reason big enough to explain it. "I wasn't in my right mind," I've imagined Mother saying. "I was so sad about your father, and then when the book was turned down, the disappointment."

In my fantasy, I respond, "The book—you mean you would have left me and Chris because of a book? He was only ten, for God's

Brookdale farm in Pennington, New Jersey, in the 1930s

*Agnes Kramer at
her wedding in 1900*

Ethel Kramer in the 1920s

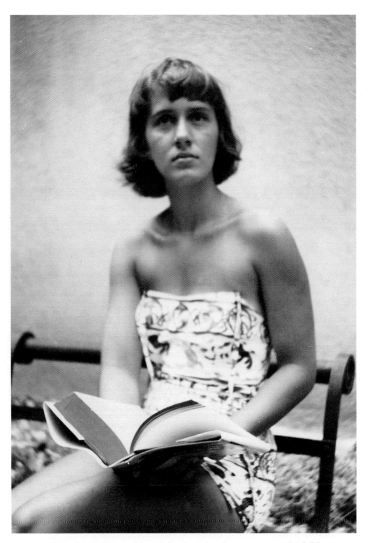

Brenda in Taos, New Mexico, in the summer of 1955

*Wolf Schwabacher
in the early 1930s*

*Brenda with her mother Ethel
at the farm, about 1938*

*Brenda with her father Wolf
in Provincetown, Massachusetts, in 1941*

*Brenda and her brother
Christopher, around 1941*

*Brenda with Connie Buttinger,
about 1942*

Brenda at home in New York, around 1948

Brenda in Berkeley, around 1968

Richard on Viale Michelangelo in Florence just after Lisa's birth, in 1963

Brenda with Lisa and Michael in the Borghese Gardens, Rome, in 1966

Michael, Lisa, and Rebecca Webster in Berkeley in 1976

Portrait of Arshile Gorky,
1972, by Ethel Schwabacher

Ethel Schwabacher in Berkeley in 1976

sake. I mean, you had friends, you had a shrink six days a week, you had Weasal, you had money and an apartment on Park Avenue, and good food and beautiful art and books. Couldn't you have found some other way to manage? Did you have to go gulping down sleeping pills? Did you think about how I'd feel coming in and trying to wake you up? You're so sensitive about things your mother did to you forty years ago—well, did you think about that?"

"She glares at me when I'm eating," I complain to Bornstein. "It makes me want to throw up. And when she isn't worrying that I'll send her to the loony bin, she just ignores me. I don't matter to her at all. Nothing I do matters. I hate her."

Bornstein murmurs sympathetically and rubs her head.

"I know I'm a bitch," I moan. "I provoke her, but I can't help it. Am I going crazy too?"

"Don't castigate yourself so much," she'd say.

But I couldn't stop feeling guilty.

Betty Parsons, owner of the famous Parsons Gallery, visited Mother in the hospital and offered her a show in the spring; this act may have saved Mother's life. She started painting again. Betty was a maverick, a woman from a wealthy family who found her true vocation as the center of the emerging group of new artists, the Abstract Expressionists. Mother's plight, beautiful and forlorn on her hospital bed, appealed to Betty. She had discovered Gorky after his death and made the characteristically brusque comment, "He was so great. Why couldn't he have stuck around?" She wanted to make sure that Mother, unlike Gorky, kept on going. When she and Mother became friends, Betty had been director of her Fifty-seventh Street gallery since 1946. The names of her artists read like a roster of Who's Who in Abstract Expressionism and included painters like Jackson Pollock, Mark Rothko, and Hans Hofmann. She created and dominated the New York art scene for some three decades.

Betty's gallery was the first to provide pure, large, open, brightly lit spaces and bone white walls for the new, often large canvases of abstract art. Mother's stripping down of her living room echoed what Betty had done with her gallery, even to the lack of concern for comfort. Betty had purposely excluded chairs and couches for visitors, to keep the focus on the paintings.

Betty often came over for lunch and I was fascinated by her husky voice and the energetic way she strode around the room. Her hair was in a long pageboy, and she would push it back when she got excited, reminding me of Ingrid Bergman in *Joan of Arc*. I saw Betty as a sort of warrior for Art, armored in sensible shoes and tailored suit. But Betty didn't have Joan's deadly seriousness: her penetrating blue eyes often had a wry humor in them. I had no idea that she was a lesbian, a lover of beautiful women like her friend Greta Garbo.

Once when Mother showed her a new painting, Betty slammed one fist into her palm. "That's terrific, Ethel, really terrific," she said in that gruff way she had, the words like little barks. "That might just well be one of the most aggressive paintings of the twentieth century. Damn," she said for emphasis. "Damn."

If Mother could paint with such strength, it seemed to me that with a little effort or will she could "snap out of it" and just be normal. I couldn't say that—she would have been hurt and furious—so instead I just kept fighting with her about trifles. It was a little like walking in a bog. Each time I tried to fight free, I sank deeper.

In April, Ed came back on leave. I saw how handsome he was, how his Navy blues fit him like a glove. We walked in Central Park by the reservoir. The night was warm, the water glimmering with reflected light from the streetlamps. Ed led me off the path under the cherry trees by the edge of the reservoir. The blossoms were almost cloyingly sweet. We stopped, Ed leaned me back against a tree, and we kissed passionately. I felt the rough bark through my dress.

Then he was pushing my skirt up. Being out there in the park where anyone could walk by and see us added to the thrill. Briefly, I saw myself in a movie, the sailor's girl. Then it happened. Ed lifted me up and guided himself between my legs. My weight did the rest. There was a moment of intense pain, then he pulled out and came into his handkerchief. The whole thing took only a minute. Blood trickled down my leg.

This was the moment my psychiatrist, my mother, and my reading of Lawrence had been pushing me toward. I'd followed my instincts and finally lost my virginity.

The experience was anticlimactic, at best. I'd wanted what Lawrence had promised and what I'd been writing about—ecstasy flowing from the throats of birds, love that overflowed all bounds. It never occurred to me that Lawrence might have been exaggerating. I retreated into poetry and wrote about a dead heart, illustrated with a heart cut in half and dripping blood-tears.

Ed wrote me exultantly that he was sure now that I loved him, ending, "I worship you. Forever."

When I told Mother that Ed and I had gone all the way, she conferred with Bornstein and then took me to a doctor and had me fitted with a diaphragm. When Muriel invited us to the farm on Ed's next leave, we got to sleep together in one bed, and she came in the morning to greet us—lying tousled and naked under the sheets—and ask us if we were ready for breakfast, just like an adult couple.

But I wasn't an adult, I wasn't even a mature teenager. When I went down to the farm, I wanted to play and romp around on the grass. My new diaphragm gave me cramps and the fluids kept dripping down my leg after we made love. It didn't seem fair that I had to be so uncomfortable and Ed so free. If I could have thought of a way to tell him I didn't want sex anymore, I would have.

Mother offered us one of her cameo rings to use as an engagement ring. Now I was practically Ed's property. Probably she didn't really expect us to marry. She was only attempting to regularize our situation, make it look better to anyone who noticed. Oh, yes, my daughter is engaged. This was, after all, the conservative, marrying 1950s. Even Ed's mother told him scornfully that if I'd do it with him before marriage, there'd be others. Now that she'd helped get me into this situation, Bornstein was definitely opposed to my marriage, and not because of our youth. Like many of the early analysts, she was a snob. Ed wasn't from the cultural or intellectual elite.

Before long I found a rationale for detaching myself. I wrote Ed over the summer before my senior year in high school that I didn't think we should sleep together anymore. Our relationship just seemed to be about sex, I told him, and I wanted something deeper. I wasn't sure what it was, but something was missing.

I threw myself into my duties as editor of our school magazine, *Blue Flag,* the job I'd been coveting since freshman year. My election was hotly contested by my friend Judy Johnson. "You have

Ed," she told me, her face very pale above the regulation blue smock. "You should have left this to me." The implication was that love and work didn't mix. If you had one, you didn't deserve the other. But I won by an impressive display of hands at the school assembly. Mother did a pen-and-ink sketch of me for the editorial page with big, dark eyes and an intelligent look.

While working on *Blue Flag*—the title referred to a flower in a poem by Edna St. Vincent Millay, stubbornly growing after a devastating fire—I began paying closer attention to the young artists who drifted through our house, watching how they played their roles. It's hard to imagine a time when there was so much passionate conviction about the importance of what these young men—there were almost no women—were doing. I got to see that it wasn't just Gorky or my crazy mother who cared, but a whole new generation. Art mattered.

Several artists made a strong impression on me. The first was Richard Pousette-Dart, who joined Betty's several years before Mother. There is a snapshot of him sitting in front of one of his fantastic paintings. He is wearing a short-sleeved casual shirt and khakis. His hairline is receding. His mouth is set in a firm line and his face has a romantic brooding intensity. I loved his paintings. They were like stained-glass windows, rich and thickly painted.

When Pousette-Dart came over, Mother seemed to be transformed into the person she undoubtably was when she painted behind closed doors. When she talked with him about painting or showed him her work, she wasn't depressed or absent; she bristled with electricity.

Pousette-Dart brought Mother notebooks of poems (just the way I did). They were dreamy but wordy. I didn't like them. I was jealous. I already knew that the center of her life was art, but what surprised and hurt me was that she could comfort him in ways she couldn't comfort me. She not only listened, she advised him about his life. She also helped another young painter, Yoram Kaniuk, through a painful divorce.

Mother bought Pousette-Dart's paintings and helped advance his work. Most of his difficulties were financial. Many of Mother's new friends—vulnerable and struggling to get a foothold—often didn't have enough to pay the rent. In this sense, her support could be crucial.

Giles Breen was the most peculiar of the young men Mother helped. He had a mop of thick yellow-brown hair and dressed in workman's overalls. He gave me the creeps—once he'd tried to fondle Chris's bare feet—but Mother told me that Giles's wife thought he was a genius and offered the Museum of Modern Art one of his paintings. Mother seemed amazed at her daring, but clearly wished that someone would do something similar for her.

Even the more established artists, like José Guerrero and Kenzo Okada, were glad of Mother's patronage. I remember going to Okada's bohemian walk-up in the Village and noticing how excited he and Kimi were to have us; how Kimi, seemingly desperate to please my mother, served us exotic dishes of seaweed and fish, and then, afraid we might not like her offerings, gave us a complete steak dinner.

Mother was tormented by the fact that though she supported other artists and bought their paintings, no one bought hers. "They say I don't need the money," she told me once. I thought that seemed fair enough; she didn't. What I didn't see was that she was also being deprived of recognition.

My graduation from high school in the spring of 1954 was squarely in the modernist tradition. I stood with my classmates in my white dress with white eyeletting, reciting T. S. Eliot's "The Hollow Men." Mother and Chris were sitting in the sixth row. She was wearing her garnet earrings and a jacket with embroidered bands in some ancient pattern on the sleeves and lapel.

Downsie had trained us to recite in chorus with soprano and alto parts. The added intensity this gave the words was thrilling. "We are the hollow men, we are the stuffed men," we recited, "headpieces . . . filled with straw." It seemed a very brave statement to make on the eve of our entrance to adulthood. Afterward we chanted Gerard Manley Hopkins. "How to . . . keep it, beauty, beauty, beauty . . . from vanishing away"—and again such pessimism was heady stuff— "No there's none, there's none, O no there's none,/Nor can you long be, what you now are, called fair." But more than the content, there was the way the alliterating words chimed against each other, the lovely mounting rhythms filling my mouth with pleasure. A sense that these crescendos of sound were what I wanted to make too.

When we got back from graduation, Mother gave me a strange present. She told me what had caused her rift with Grandma.

The subject came up almost by accident. Oscar Williams, a man Mother dated occasionally—mostly, as far as I could see, to talk about his dead wife—had given me a copy of his *Little Treasury of Modern Poetry* for graduation. I was pleased because he had procured a dedication from W. H. Auden, but I couldn't help making some comments about how wimpy Oscar was with his glasses and his little bow tie, always giving out free copies of his anthologies at openings.

Mother, prompted by my negative comments, reassured me that she wouldn't marry again. Ever since Mother's first show at Betty's, she'd gone out with a number of men—the good reviews made her more confident. The only one who struck me as having any juice was a criminal lawyer with piercing eyes named Alex. I suspected they slept together, but even that didn't worry me. No one could contend with my father's memory.

So I was startled when she went on to say that if she did fall in love, my inheritance would be safe. She had established a trust for me when I was born, with all the money she had brought to her marriage with my father: $10,000. She couldn't touch it.

Money was the last thing I would have thought to worry about, so I just stared at her while she told me about Grandma's second marriage, to a romantic con man she thought was a baron.

Mother's face twisted the way it did when she was angry at me. "I told her not to do it," she told me fiercely. "We were at dinner once and I looked Willy in the eye and squeezed the glass I was holding until it broke and blood ran down my arm."

"Why?" I stammered.

"To show him how much I hated him and make him leave my mother alone. But she married him, and after they were married, she signed over her fortune to him. Then he left her. It was my inheritance."

It was a little like the moment of revelation in a fairy tale. Except that I wasn't the daughter of a king, I was the granddaughter of a woman who'd been cruelly duped. The moral of the story was clear:

Be on guard. No matter how much you love a man, keep your bank accounts separate. The message—as antiromantic as you can get—was counter to all Mother's previous urgings to follow my impulses. For once, she was trying to tell me something practical—that romantic love, while wonderful, could get you into a lot of trouble. That some sort of rational control was necessary.

Much later, I found a series of letters Mother wrote to Grandma from Europe in 1928 and 1929 about Willy and money. She addresses Grandma as "Cutie," almost the way you would a child, and draws a little diagram of how her allowance should be divided into installments—"January, February, March, $1,000"—as though my grandmother were lacking any capacity to count.

Clearly money was more important to Mother than she pretended later, and I can't help noticing that $300 per month was a lot of money for those days. Probably the sum included her analysis with Dr. Deutsch. The thought of earning her own money didn't occur to her, although other women in the 1920s, including some of her friends, were doing it. When she didn't have enough money to continue her analysis, she turned to a rich uncle, David, for additional funds. The idea of an independent female simply didn't exist in our family. My daughter Lisa is the first of us to actually earn a living.

In February 1929, Mother wrote Grandma,

> Your recent letters are vague and give rise to all sorts of suspicions.
>
> What possible effect can your difference of idea as to your disposal of your own money have had on your relation with Willy's parents? I don't like it.
>
> I understood that your affairs were to be completely separate. This should be completely in the open. Every few months there seems to be a new situation. You doubt Uncle David's good sense. You doubt his lawyers, you listen politely to me, but probably doubt mine and go right ahead involving your means with Willy.
>
> You must not make mistakes that would endanger not alone James and myself and yourself but your mental happiness. The man appreciates a woman more when she has a sound sense of her own good and knows how to keep her capital intact.
>
> It is not that I distrust Willy. But for God's sake realize that being in the center of it you cannot see so clearly as the others

less attached. I do not know what in the world to say to keep you from making what they call "*des bêtises*."

love, E

P.S. I could not forgive you if you broke with Uncle David or involved your affairs. It is simply not the thing to do.

Mother was true to her word. She didn't forgive my grandmother for losing her money until Grandma was ninety. Then after years of bitterness they became friends again, and Mother helped her financially until she died in the late 1960s. By the time I was in my twenties, Mother referred to Grandma tenderly. And when I visited Grandma, she would tell me that Mother was the best of daughters. The reconciliation was one of Dr. Kris's great successes.

Mother never did marry again, though she certainly had ample opportunity. She was only forty-five when my father died. But romantics are famous for disliking the real thing. Analysis was the ideal situation for her. The love was intense, it took place through an artistic medium (words), and it was deliciously unconsummated. Dr. Kris was my mother's Beatrice, her Laura, her Lady Dulcinea. Naturally Mother avoided analyzing her dependence on Dr. Kris—why should she ruin a good thing?

Chapter

7

*The individual finds himself "free" in the
negative sense, that is, alone with his self and
confronting an alienated, hostile world. In this
situation, to quote a telling description of
Dostoyevski, in* The Brothers Karamazov, *he has
"no more pressing need than the one to find
somebody to whom he can surrender, as quickly
as possible, that gift of freedom which he, the
unfortunate creature, was born with."*

—ERICH FROMM

Swarthmore College was like a dose of strong medicine given to
a patient already weakened by disease. I was emotionally exhausted.
I burst into tears when I got a C on my first English paper because
of poor spelling. I hated tests and couldn't seem to get the facts to
stick in my head.

I had gotten away from Mother, Ed, and Bornstein to a place
filled with trees and flowers and incredibly stimulating students, but
the work was demanding—and, unlike at Dalton, graded. I was
marked down for lacking the skills I had ignored at my high
school—and I was supposed to manage myself as a young adult.

In all fairness to Dalton I eventually got the hang of it academi-
cally, and did as well as people with more disciplined schooling. But
I was still a white rabbit in a field full of dogs. It was only natural
that I attracted an upperclassman hunting for a suitably malleable
girlfriend. David was a philosophy student with wire-rimmed glasses and unkempt curly hair. We spent days discussing Bishop Berkeley and whether the world really existed. I enjoyed these talks. Philosophy had so few facts to remember and took place in a
comfortingly ideal realm.

If I'd been another sort of person, Swarthmore might have
marked my beginning as an activist, or even a terrorist. David surrounded himself with campus radicals who led protests and shared
a dislike of the upper classes. They referred to me, only half joking,
as "that rich Park Avenue bitch."

I was too beset by my inner turmoils to think about changing the world. I let myself go physically, calling Mother from the phone booth in our drafty dorm hall to complain about my sore throats or ask her how to cope with my life. I realized that my concerns went straight to Dr. Kris, but I didn't find this strange. By now I was used to having my problems scrutinized by experts.

By spring of my freshman year, my health was better and my spirits lifted by the daffodils thrusting up exuberantly along the walks. After a few minutes of studying, David would touch my thigh, and before long we'd be lying out under the lilac bushes, fooling around. David was a sophisticated lover compared to Ed. What he liked best was to arouse me until I insisted on going back to the dorm, putting in my diaphragm, and making love. Though I still didn't have orgasms, I was getting close, and was fascinated by the new sensations that flooded my body. I begged him to show me what he was doing so I could try it myself.

After an outdoor episode on a warm night, in which we'd gotten a little careless, my period was late. I was overwhelmed by anxiety. In my art history class, while the professor showed slides of Thomas poking his doubting finger in Christ's wounds, I would surreptitiously stick a finger under the edge of my underwear through the hole in my pocket, then withdraw it and stick it in my mouth. No blood. Maybe it was late because David had crashed his scooter the week before and we'd narrowly escaped being killed. Maybe my system was on some sort of general strike. I would try to concentrate, but nothing the professor said made any sense.

I waited two weeks to get a test. I called from the phone in the dorm hallway. Outside the window, a forsythia was in bloom. "It's positive," a woman's voice said. "Congratulations!" Congratulations. I imagined my father looking down at me, disappointed and angry at my lack of care for myself. Why couldn't I have said, "No, I have to study" when David asked me to sneak off behind the library for a quick snuggle? And why hadn't I carried my diaphragm with me in my book bag?

In so far as I was a female Everywoman, this was the end of the Permissive Road. I'd reached the bog. But as always, the guides who had encouraged me along the way—Mother and Kris and Bornstein—were there to help me through it.

Mother never reproached me; she just hugged me and told me not to worry, she'd get me an abortion, it would be all right. I went to my child analyst to talk it over. Bornstein didn't want me to think I had to have an abortion. I could have the baby if I wanted. I was lucky, she said, to have such an understanding mother who let me make up my own mind. David came to New York with me, and we saw Bornstein together. He told her that he loved me and would marry me. He was bright and radical to boot, and she found him suitable enough.

Like many other teenagers who accidentally get pregnant, I actually yearned for a baby. I liked the idea of having a small creature growing inside me. Someone dependent on me, completely my own. Even the fact that my breasts were beginning to swell gave me an inexplicable satisfaction. But I was no more ready to marry and care for a baby than I was to fly. I still hadn't the slightest idea of how to get along with another person. I was a caldron of unmet needs. Seeing David playing ball with his brother in Washington Square Park sent me into a jealous rage. Once at the beach with his family, I had become so angry at losing his attention—he was being particularly loving to his mother—that I let myself get terribly sunburned, finally getting what I wanted: David sat by my bed murmuring sympathetically while he put cold compresses on my blistered face.

In the 1950s, before you could have a legal abortion, you had to see two psychiatrists who would certify that you might harm yourself if you weren't allowed to have one. Bornstein explained this to me, pressing the cold glass to her head the way she always did when she was worried. I didn't want to have the baby, I said finally, feeling at once guilty but suddenly sure of myself. I wanted to go back to college. To my surprise, I wanted passionately to finish my schooling now that it was threatened. (If students married and had a baby at Swarthmore, one of them, usually the girl, had to leave.) This was the first real feeling of something I wanted for myself.

Mother was unusually kind. She let me talk to her about my increased appetite and morning sickness and, most important, she called the doctor who would do the abortion.

"He thought, from the way I was talking, you must be only twelve," she said with a laugh when she put down the receiver. "He was relieved to hear you were eighteen." Our family doctor was much less tolerant. He told her I was just too hot to let loose, that she should marry me off. She repeated this to me; I think she wanted to show me she was on my side even if most people wouldn't be.

In order to have my abortion, I had to act the crazy girl that I was so afraid of being. The first doctor had a nervous tic in his eye and seemed more afraid of me than I was of him. I sat, twisting my handkerchief between my fingers while he asked me what I was going to do. "I don't know," I kept repeating, "I just don't know," making my voice more ominous with every repetition. It worked. Bornstein told me that the doctor had found me terribly disturbed. I was shocked. Didn't he know that I was acting: that this was just a charade that every girl had to go through to get an abortion? Or could he see that I really was a mental case?

The second psychiatrist was a friend of Muriel and my father. I didn't pretend with him. I just told him I felt terrible. The kinder the doctor was, the worse I felt.

Before the operation I had to spend a day at Bellevue on the mental ward. Doctors came by with young interns and pulled up my nightgown, and everyone stared and poked my belly as if I were one of Charcot's hysterics. I wrote David a long letter about this and about the white-gowned women who crept through the halls. Later, my mother told me that to protect me she'd torn up the letter instead of delivering it to David, as I'd asked. This was something to be forgotten, not recorded, she insisted. I never thought to ask her what she was doing, reading my mail.

By the time I was ready to go back to college, I had missed a month of classes. I remember sitting in my flowery pink bedroom when Bornstein visited me at home. She told me that she thought I ought to take a semester off. I might not do well on my exams, I told her, but I was going back. I didn't want to stop, even for a semester. I wouldn't. Underneath, I was afraid that Mother wouldn't have minded if I fell apart, that she wanted me home at any cost. If I gave up my foothold at Swarthmore—my separate place—I'd be engulfed by her growing needs.

To explain my weakness, I told people that I had a bleeding ulcer. My professors were lenient with me. David let me hand in one of his seminar papers as my own. Ironically, the paper was on ethics, and, of course, I got an A. My political science professor let me take my exam in my room, and Mother actually came down to school and sat with me, buying me chocolate milkshakes to keep up my strength. I barely passed some of my courses, but I hadn't cracked up and hadn't stayed home.

That summer provided a coda to my flirtation with disaster: I met Frieda, the widow of my hero, D. H. Lawrence, the prophet of sex as ultimate fulfillment. Mother had decided to spend the summer in Taos, New Mexico, sharing a house with a novelist friend of hers, Lenore Marshall. Mother was going to paint and work on her Gorky book. She was due to have a second solo show at Betty's in February of 1956, as well as a painting in the Whitney Annual Exhibition of Contemporary Art in November.

D. H. Lawrence had been invited to Taos in the 1920s by Mabel Dodge Luhan, a rich eccentric American who dreamed of founding an artistic community that would revitalize American art. In 1922 Lawrence joined her in Taos with Frieda; Mabel Dodge, who had married the Pueblo Indian Tony Luhan, built him a house near the pueblo. In his letters, Lawrence talks excitedly about the Indians' wild dances and his hopes for a new antimaterialist society where people would act not from their heads, but from their solar plexuses.

Frieda met us at the door of her adobe and ushered us in. She must have been nearly eighty, but she radiated sexual energy and had a full, rich, deeply accented voice. I felt faint, I was so excited at seeing her, but I revived when she showed Mother the brightly colored paintings that hung around the little living room. "Lorenzo's paintings," she said in her wonderful voice. They were large full-bodied nudes, clearly of him and her. It was almost too much for me, but Mother took it with her usual regal politeness. Then we looked at Lawrence's collected works on the bookshelf, bound in leather with gold lettering on the covers. Every time Frieda said the word "Lorenzo" it sounded like a caress. Afterwards, we had tea outside. I sat reverentially at Frieda's feet. A stocky Indian, whom she introduced to us only as Antonio, gave me a ceramic brooch he had made, glazed with blue and gold.

I was grateful to Mother for introducing me to Frieda, but I was also angry at her for dragging me to New Mexico, where I was lonely and out of sorts. In one letter to David, I compared Mother to a vampire. Another time I awakened from a nightmare to find myself biting and kicking her as she tried to soothe me.

"One sheds one's sickness in books," Lawrence said somewhere. In our dead white adobe, I tried to begin a realistic autobiographical novel. But too much was clogging my mind: death, pregnancy, suicide attempts. I couldn't sort it out, much less express and master it. Besides, my mother's romantic vision continued to exert a seductive counterpull.

"Look at that purple on the mountain," she would say. "Can you see the flecks of gold in it? Isn't it glorious?"

I would look and see only a faint haze of color, sage, and rock. What was the matter with me? Why couldn't I see in the intense, almost febrile way she did? Why weren't the mountains moving and glowing, the rainclouds pulsing blackness? Why were my perceptions so small and ordinary compared to hers?

Romantic passion was in everything she did. After the visit to the site of Lawrence's primitivist dreams, Mother took me to a conference on desegregation. It was 1955, less than a year after the Supreme Court decision. She had joined the Urban League to keep up with my father's interests, but whereas his approach was practical, she saw blacks as engaged in a heroic struggle and would later embody it in a series of epic paintings. I tagged along to the conference and took notes for a paper at school.

Afterward, Mother decided to cheer me up by sending me for a week to a utopian farm run by some friends of hers, a famous neurologist and his wife who swam naked in their lake and raised their own food. The nudist farm made me want to figure out my position. Could utopias (sexual, artistic, liberal) really work? I was surrounded by idealists, but looking at myself made me pessimistic. I wanted to be generous but felt cramped and tight, and my motives seemed to center on my own survival.

Back at Swarthmore in the fall, I signed up for Mr. March's "History of Ideas" and wrote a paper on B. F. Skinner's behaviorist utopia, *Walden Two*. He thought you could rid children of their negative emotions through education. By now I had begun to read and appreciate Freud, who said you could suppress jealousy and hate but not change them.

After an excruciating week in which Mr. March assigned a thousand pages of reading, I cheated on my midterm. I sat on the toilet in a bathroom cubicle and studied the notes that I'd secreted behind the trash basket. I remember I was afraid of being caught and expelled in disgrace, but I didn't feel any guilt. I'd done all the reading, hadn't I? It didn't seem fair that my anxiety had kept me from retaining it.

Somehow David had an easier time managing both sex and work. Even when we fought, which we did more and more, he could switch to Kant without missing a beat.

By now my love life was a mess. I hadn't been willing to marry David, but I was still going with him. And besides him, I had a premed student at Harvard who thought he was pinned to me. And Ed—now a pilot-in-training for the Navy—had somehow managed to hang on, writing me from flight school that he still wanted to marry me. I didn't want any of them, but I wouldn't let any of them go.

When I went back midyear to see Mother's show at Betty's, I visited Bornstein, who shocked me by telling me, after I had admitted my confusion, that I was a "sick" girl and needed help. I found out later that Mother had told Bornstein that some friends had seen me riding on a scooter at school dressed in black leather and urged her to bring me back before I went off the deep end. Bornstein believed that I should come home and be analyzed for real. She thought I should change now to a male analyst. If I wanted, she would help me find someone suitable.

I looked at Mother's paintings' brilliant—almost cheerful—colors and wondered if Mother's therapy had helped her. She wasn't trying to kill herself anymore. And she seemed to be getting along better with Grandma—acknowledged her as a source of her art. Though when I thought about it, concentrating on the past seemed to leech Mother's energy from the present. She made every effort to contact her childhood, but taking a five-minute taxi ride to meet me at the gallery was still too much trouble.

What decided the issue was the collapse of my roommate, Starr. Starr was a waifish, witty blonde who wanted to be a painter and spent most of her time seducing her professors. One afternoon, I came in late to find her stark naked, smoothing an Indian bedspread over pillows she'd stacked on the floor. When I asked her if she was planning to sleep on the floor, she smirked at me oddly.

"Can't you see it's an altar?" she asked, adjusting the gold candlesticks on either side of the pillows. They had tall black candles in them.

"It's to Baudelaire, the divine master," she said amiably, sitting cross-legged in front of her altar and starting to intone lines from *Les Fleurs du mal.*

"Very funny," I said and then I realized it wasn't a joke. Sweat beaded on her lower lip, but the skin on her arms was covered with gooseflesh. While she chanted *"hypocrite lecteur—mon semblable—mon frère,"* I threw a bathrobe over her shoulders.

A few days later she rushed into our room and collapsed on her bed panting. She looked terrible. Her skin was clammy. She lay there with her eyes closed, tossing back and forth on the bed.

"He's a shit," she moaned.

"I'm sure he is," I said, trying to remember which love affair she was on. I offered to get her an aspirin or, better, the gin bottle at the bottom of her underwear drawer. But she waved me away.

"I was walking at the edge of the train platform, and the bloody walls started closing in on me. Can you imagine how that feels?"

I almost could, which scared me.

The next week I woke before dawn to hear Starr giggling. A naked black man was staring at me from Starr's bed, white teeth bared in a grin.

"You know you talk in your sleep?" Starr said, raising herself to a sitting position and giggling inanely, "and you snore . . . like this." She gave a rattling imitation and collapsed backward into her friend's arms.

This was too much. I bought earplugs and eyeshades, but it didn't work. I lay awake wondering when the next guy was going to sneak into her room. I finally went to the dean of women and told her that Starr was having problems that I couldn't handle; I needed a single room. She was a good-natured Southern lady. She lectured me for ten minutes on how we had a duty to take care of our fellows. "It's paaat of thu luhning experience, don't yawl see?"

David thought that Mother was coming between him and me.

"How? How?" I'd ask.

"I don't know," he'd insist stubbornly, "but every time you visit, you come back in tatters. It's as though there's a wall of glass between us. I can't get through to you. I know it's her."

"It's not, it's Starr. It's my crazy roommate. Why do you say things like that?"

"Look," he said finally. "Maybe I'm wrong. Come with me to Europe this summer. We need time to ourselves."

"Okay," I said, burrowing my head against his chest. I had a vision of us riding around on a scooter, my arms around his waist, learning to be a couple.

When I told Mother our plan, she didn't say no outright. She didn't need to. First, she subtly undermined the idea by reminding me of my scooter accident and delicately wondering if David had enough money to afford a trip like this. When that didn't work, she invited us to come to Provincetown with her footing the bill. "You can be by yourselves as much as you want."

Her voice was soft. Did I only imagine the threat under the softness? Of rage against me or violence against herself? David was incredulous that I'd given in without a fight.

"We can fish, sail . . . it's beautiful there," my voice trailed off lamely. "I'd feel like a bitch if I deserted her."

"She's the bitch, don't you see? She's manipulating you shamelessly." But I refused to see—"You're cruel," I screamed. "All she wants is company"—and in the end, I wore him down.

Before we left for the Cape, Mother went with David to Tiffany's and helped him pick out an engagement ring for me, a brilliant amethyst. She thought we should be engaged formally so that if I got pregnant again it would seem natural to marry. I didn't want to be engaged, I wanted to be in Europe with David joyriding on a red scooter. But though I could fight with her about small matters, with a major one, as David noted bitterly, I simply went limp.

Toward the end of the summer, during which David and I made love every night in a room adjoining Mother's, I was accepted as a transfer student at Barnard. I would be back in New York, living at home, just as Mother wanted. That way, as Mother pointed out to me, I'd be closer to David, who was starting medical school at Yale. And I could start a real analysis just like hers.

"You always said I should get rid of my witch and get a real shrink," I wrote Starr, who was recovering from her breakdown. "Well, I have—he's tall, dark, and handsome and I start in September." I didn't mention David once.

Chapter

8

*Eissler was . . . (and remains) one of the grand
old men of contemporary psychoanalysis. He is
tall, gaunt, and unmistakably European. He
speaks with an accent whose dominant tone of
Viennese asperity is incongruously coupled with
and . . . rendered all but pointless by an
underlying, insistent, almost pathological
kindheartedness. There is a class of people,
however, to whom this kindheartedness does not
extend. These are the enemies of Sigmund Freud.*
—Janet Malcolm

The most interesting character in my life in the fall of 1956 was
my new therapist, Kurt Eissler. At least he was the biggest influence
in *Liebe* and *Arbeit,* as Freud says. Eissler lived at 300 Central Park
West, right across the park from me. At our first meeting to see if
we could work together, I noticed that his waiting room was filled
with reproductions of famous statues. Nefertiti's head and a beautiful bronze cat were my favorites. The apartment looked right, even
smelled right, fresh flowers tempering the musty smells of papers
and books.

Eissler was Bornstein's friend as well as Muriel's; they had all
been in Vienna together. He had a golden cocker spaniel that looked
exactly like Bornstein's—the dogs were from the same litter. When I
told him how upset I had been about Bornstein's birthmark, he
smiled. "The children often say she looks like a witch." He spoke,
like her, with a heavy German accent, enunciating carefully as if he
had difficulty getting his tongue around the English sounds. He was
black-haired and handsome in an intellectual way. There was a suggestion of puritanism about him—in his earnestness and his steel-
rimmed glasses—but there was also a sensuality. The bottom part of
his face with its very full lips seemed to express a different personality from the intellectual top half.

He was already a well-known analyst and Freud's fervent champion. As founder of the Freud Archives, he had boxes full of historic documents and records on his top shelves. I didn't know anything about the struggles within and around the movement, but it was impossible not to sense his commitment. If Freud was King Arthur, Eissler was Launcelot, a quixotic but fiercely loyal defender of the faith.

When some years later a sociologist named Paul Roazen wrote a book blaming Freud for the death of one of his disciples, Victor Tausk, Eissler dashed off an entire book defending the master. Still later, there was the notorious conflict between Eissler and Jeffrey Masson, a brilliant young analyst he'd befriended. Eissler had proposed Masson as his successor as head of the archives, but when Masson criticized Freud for abandoning his seduction theory, Eissler fired him. Masson—out of a prestigious job and incensed at the censorship—sued Eissler. In 1983, Janet Malcolm's series of *New Yorker* articles, "Trouble in the Archives," made Masson seem opportunistic and Eissler inflexible and gullible. Though I'd finished therapy with Eissler years earlier and was aware of some of his shortcomings by then, I was sorry for him.

Eissler may have been orthodox and inflexible (as Janet Malcolm and Jeffrey Masson suggest), but I was drawn in by his kindness. We decided right away that I would start with three times a week and that I would lie on the couch. When my brother started his analysis at Harvard, he told me his analyst said the treatment would take at least seven years, but I don't recall Eissler telling me anything like that. It strikes me now that he didn't really consider it an analysis, but more a palliative therapy to keep me going until I was well enough to leave home. The main things he concentrated on in the sessions were my fights with my mother, which he insisted I had to stop before we could get anywhere, and my sex life. Being an orthodox Freudian he tried hard to connect my high degree of anxiety with conflict over sex. He thought my perpetual sore throats (and hypochondria), for example, were a result of having oral sex. Like Freud, he probably considered oral sex a deviation from the goal of mature genitality. At any rate, Eissler pictured my throat as reacting like a Victorian maiden, blushing red in outrage at the noxious sperm.

I liked Eissler much better than I had Bornstein and didn't find my free associations blocked by obsessive thoughts. It was fun to talk to him about sex and see how intent he got, but nonetheless I remember holding back when I got to specific sexual thoughts about him. Once, for example, when I was having trouble studying because of some construction going on outside my apartment, he offered me some earplugs, standing up and walking around to me on the couch. His fly was about level with my face and I remember associating the round wax earplugs with the view of his testicles I'd see if I unzipped it. I would have died rather than say this to him. But I can see now that holding back meant I never really analyzed my feelings for him. And I don't think he analyzed his for me. It was a bit odd for an orthodox analyst to be offering his patient earplugs or books or any of the other little things he gave me.

Unlike Bornstein, who hadn't mentioned dreams, Eissler encouraged me to bring mine in regularly. I'd read Freud's *Interpretation of Dreams* and kept waiting for an orderly progression of associations leading to understanding of some conflict or problem, but I was always disappointed. Eissler was too. "Your dreams seem like little short stories," he complained, "not dreams at all." In other words, he couldn't make anything of them.

Meanwhile, I lived at home and commuted to Morningside Heights every day by bus. Barnard was a relief from the pressures of Swarthmore. I had the probably unfair impression that many of the nice Jewish girls at my new school sat around knitting and waiting for a husband.

Luckily, Judy Johnson had transferred from Radcliffe the same year (her husband, Jimmy, was working in the city) and we picked up where we left off. I switched from philosophy to English and joined the Barnard magazine. Our year was a particularly good one for writers. In addition to Judy, who was still some years away from winning the Yale Younger Poets prize, we had Norma Klein and Tobi Bernstein, Janet Burroway, Rosellen (Posie) Brown, and Lynne Sharon Schwartz. Norma and Tobi both became writers of children's books. Norma's most popular was probably *Mom, the Wolf Man and Me.* Tobi wrote books about her passion, ballet. Janet, Rosellen, and Lynne became distinguished writers of literary fiction.

Though I liked the others, Judy was still my closest literary friend. We took several courses together. My impulses were still toward romanticism, but the Romantic poets were taught by a spinsterish, older woman named Eleanor who managed to drain all the excitement out of them. Judy sat in the back writing poetry while I fantasized about whether Byron really had incest with his sister. After that, Judy persuaded me to take Mr. Robertson's Shakespeare. I got the highest mark in the class simply because of my good short-term memory. We were supposed to identify lines from the plays and I was the only one who remembered that "Anon, anon, Francis" was a remark to a servant in *Henry V*. Clearly Barnard was going to be easy. And with David off at Yale, I was able to concentrate. My grades shot up from low Bs to As. I made the dean's list.

I also found my first real mentor, Rosalie Colie, a brilliant woman, small and sharp with dark flashing eyes, who taught the metaphysical poets and Milton. She had been a roommate of my father's secretary Ann Dix, knew all about our family tragedies, and had an inclination to be kind to me. She encouraged my fascination with the way the metaphysical poets connected body and spirit. I developed a passion for Donne's poems addressed to God. Lines like "breake, blowe, burn and make me new" made me feel the possibility of transformation. Unfortunately, I had no God to "batter my heart" into the proper condition. I had only Dr. Eissler.

In my sessions, I recounted my almost daily fights with Mother.

"You must try to stop acting out," he told me. "How can all this make you feel better?"

It didn't. It was terrible. In a foggy way I felt that though the fights seemed to be my fault they weren't entirely. They were part of my history with her. Now, I think that Mother's earlier rages and coldness had built up a reservoir of anger and fear that made me provoke her. In a way, it meant that I was orchestrating her moods, and therefore was no longer at their mercy. It was like setting off a display of fireworks. But by her anxious hovering and intrusions, she provoked me in ways I wasn't aware of (and Eissler didn't explore). She liked to have me weak and dependent—if I'd been a star, it would have threatened her. Often by talking about the achievements of other people's children, for example, she subtly undercut what little confidence I had. Feeling hurt but not understanding why, I would react by quarreling over achievement as a value.

None of this was clear to me then. All I knew was that when she came into the room and asked me how I felt, or how I'd slept or what I was doing, a dark sullen mood settled over my heart. Even if I'd been humming to myself the moment before she came, the song dried up and I had to complain about something. "My bones ache," I would say with grim satisfaction. "I think I have a fever. I'll flunk for sure." My complaints were like a fist hitting her again and again, but I didn't feel too bad about it because they hit me too. Eissler's telling me to stop didn't help at all.

Curious about how therapy was supposed to work, I got Eissler's book *The Psychiatrist and the Dying Patient* out of the library and devoured it in one sitting. It was an astonishing book in which, very like a priest, he tried to help his dying charges to a new stage of awareness. There was a woman whose controlling husband insisted she dress like a doll and who, at the point she decided she was ready to live her own life, got cancer. With Eissler's help, she went on to live as fully as she could in the short time remaining. Another, younger woman, a mother and a doctor, had to cope not only with premature death and sorrow over leaving her children but with anger at her internist for misdiagnosing her.

What was instructive about their stories for me was how these women dealt with suffering and imminent death. They didn't go crazy and rave like Mother; they actually used their pain to grow. The young doctor not only forgave her internist but found a loving nanny for her children, someone they could get accustomed to before their mother died. I was awed by her integrity and strength.

"I don't see how that woman could think so much about her children when she was dying," I told Eissler. I couldn't even concentrate when my throat hurt.

"We know your mother wasn't a good model for you in this," he said, clicking his tongue disapprovingly, "giving all her energies to her art when you were small."

If Mother had been a man, Eissler would have endorsed her passion for her art, but she was a woman. He had clear ideas about how women should feel and behave, and Mother didn't fit them. For one thing, women should care first about their children. For another thing, there could be no feminine genius. Later, I found out that Mother thought she was cursed by being a genius trapped in the body of a woman. Eissler, though he worshiped genius with the same fervor as he worshiped Freud, felt it could only come in male containers. At the most, a woman could hope to be the wife of a great man.

He spent a good deal of our time gently probing to see if I had the capacity to be the wife of a genius. He would tell me what Mrs. Tolstoy had to put up with—with her more than ten pregnancies and her husband's turn to religion—and wonder if I had that kind of endurance.

Eissler himself was working on Shakespeare, the greatest genius of them all, and had chosen the Bard's most enigmatic work, *Hamlet*, to illuminate. Not only had *Hamlet* been one of psychoanalysis's urtexts, illustrating Oedipal conflicts, but the question of Hamlet's madness or sanity was one that had baffled critics for centuries. Eissler projected a huge work, using all that had been said and thought before, that would finally get to the bottom of Hamlet's character.

When I told him about a paper I was writing on the paradox of reason-in-madness in *King Lear,* it was so near his own subject that Eissler couldn't resist giving me his opinions, not only about Lear's regressed state but about his daughter Cordelia. Eissler was impressed by Cordelia's honesty. I was annoyed by her misleading bluntness. I think she's rather perverse, I said, why can't she reassure the old man? Because this is about reality, he said, not reassurance. This led us to a discussion of the roles of children and parents and what happens when the roles are reversed and a parent gives up power prematurely. I suppose it was as good a way as any of getting at my issues, but I also think I was a good sounding board for his ideas. After that, I regularly told him about my paper—which ended up being cited by my mentor, Miss Colie, in her book on paradox— while Eissler, for his part, would come into my sessions full of excitement about indications in Hamlet's soliloquies of his growing maturity. I was flattered. He seemed to be taking me seriously.

But I was also confused. Was I supposed to develop my mind, or train myself to be a sort of high-grade domestic as the wife of a genius? Trying to figure it out, I wrote a story called "The Garden and the Sea." Its heroine was a young painter of sexualized Lawrentian flowers who couldn't cope with either the demands of life or love and drowned herself by walking into the sea. Reading it now, I see the story was about the dangers of identifying with my mother.

"I don't want you to send this out," Mother said, when I gave her the story to read. "It will lead to talk."

"But lots of people kill themselves," I said ingenuously, "like Virginia Woolf. Besides, my heroine has a boyfriend just like David. If anything, people will think it's about me." David and I were in the process of breaking up. Every time I went up to Yale to visit him, we fought.

"I'm sorry," Mother said darkly. We were sitting together on my bed. "But you just can't do it. Put it on the shelf and work on something else."

I could have sent the story out and not told her about it, but I wanted her to like it, to tell me it was okay to write anything I pleased.

One day soon after I showed Mother my story, I found her lying across her bed crying. When I touched her shoulder and asked her what was the matter, she turned away from me, pressing her face into the tufted white spread. Finally, she sat up and let me get her a glass of water.

"My brother died," she said when she'd taken a sip. The flap of her dress jacket was turned back and the crimson silk inside made me think of blood.

"What?" I stammered, "What brother? You don't have a brother."

"Yes, I do," she said, not looking at me. "Your Uncle James. He was in an institution. I didn't want to disturb you." It all tumbled out through her tears. As a young man, he'd been a brilliant mathematician, then inexplicably gone crazy. She was still in awe of his phenomenal mind.

Not "disturb" me to find out I had a mad, brilliant, thoroughly dead uncle? It was almost funny. I felt like a small pond the cows had walked through.

No wonder she'd never shown me any photo albums, no pictures from her childhood. I made her give me Grandma's photo album—the one, ironically, Grandma had assembled for Jimmy as a child. I wanted to see what my mother's hidden brother looked like, but I also wanted to check to make sure no one else was missing. A set of Siamese twins? An elephant-headed boy?

I went through the book slowly. There was Jimmy as a baby in what looked like a christening dress, beautifully embroidered with lace, held by his great-grandfather Meyers.

The next pictures showed Jimmy as a one-year-old, still in a dress, this time with a silk bow in the center, a beautiful baby with intense dark eyes, one fist clenched, looking slightly startled. A few pages further, Jimmy, around ten, dressed in dark wool knickers and a long jacket with a white shirt and tie, sat on one arm of his father's chair looking rather sadly at a book Grandpa was reading. My mother—ravishing with her dark hair topped by a huge bow and a low-belted dress like Dorothy in Oz—had her arm possessively around her father's neck and was staring passionately into his face. There were a few more shots of Jimmy. Then, after one last photo of him at camp as a young adolescent, he vanished.

"He pulled me around by the hair when I was a child," Mother said, when I asked her what Jimmy was like. "My mother always thought it was funny, but he was hurting me."

"I'm sorry," I said, picturing her with her eyes screwed up, her scalp burning as Jimmy tugged. I asked Mother when Jimmy went crazy. Not until his late twenties, she told me. When he was a child he had been considered a genius—this she told me with a grimace, half pride, half rivalrous fury. He had gotten a Ph.D. in engineering from MIT. She had tried to find him help, but it was no good; nothing worked. I tried to hold her hand; she was sitting on her bed with her books next to her and the little bell she used for calling Weasal, but she pulled away. "Never mind, darling," she said. But her voice sounded helpless, and all the images she gave me were already lying inside me like some huge, indigestible meal.

Much later, in California, after I became friends with my poet cousin George Oppen and his wife, Mary, I asked them if they remembered this mysterious uncle. Mary knew Jimmy in New York, she said. He fell in love with a friend of hers in the Village. He brought her odd gifts: a cord of firewood, a canary. And, she added, he liked to fly kites—in the winter, over the snow.

I looked at the photos again. Jimmy's eyes seemed heavy-lidded, his mouth turned down at the corners while my mother's gaze was alternately fierce, sullen, or passionately demanding. But there wasn't enough to go on. If I wanted to know more about him, I would have to invent it.

Secrets necessitate other secrets until a whole separate life is going on, on the other side of a curtain. After my mother died in 1984, my brother got a phone call from a woman who said she was Uncle James's daughter. I met Cecilia at Mother's retrospective show in Albany. She was a pleasant woman with dark hair and eyes who looked a little like me. A social worker. Married to a Greek named Soulis. She had one child, a son named James.

She asked shyly if I had any pictures of her father. He divorced her mother when Cecilia was very small, and she wanted to know what he looked like. Incredible as it seemed, my mother had been in contact with Cecilia and not only had never told us about her but had kept her from seeing Grandma.

"She told me Agnes has enough grandchildren," Cecilia said sadly.

"Why?" I asked my brother after the show.

"Mother thought they weren't classy enough," my brother said, only half joking.

When I told Eissler about Jimmy, he was curiously silent. He wouldn't tell me what he thought about the possibility that I had inherited some genetic instability, resorting to the classic "What do you think?" whenever I brought it up. My conclusion was that there was in fact some inherited weakness in the basic fabric that predisposed us to crazing—like badly fired ceramic pots. I comforted myself with the bromides Dr. Kris fed Mother: that Mother was not as sick as her brother, that my brother, Chris, and I were healthier still, and that since the generations were improving, there was a good chance that our children, if we had them, would be only mildly neurotic.

Despite his patriarchal ideas, Eissler encouraged my writing, just as he encouraged me when I took acting senior year with Mildred Dunnock and thought briefly of a career on the stage. He introduced me to an editor named Seymour Copstein, who sent my suicide story to a friend of his who was the editor of *Playboy*—but it was definitely not *Playboy* material and nothing came of it. I kept seeing Seymour, though, because he helped me structure my college papers.

Then, one day, he showed me his fussily decorated bedroom, explaining that his wife was "a Victorian lady," and asked if I knew how he felt about me. "Like a father?" I said, hopefully. I was always looking for fathers. He grabbed me and started to kiss me. I pulled away and ran out the door.

Eissler was unsympathetic. He said that I was quite unconscious of the provocative things I did, that I was probably leaning on the table in an enticing way. Besides, he said, there was no way that he, Eissler, could have foreseen this. Even Freud, he told me shrugging his shoulders, wasn't a *Menschenkenner*—a judge of men.

Now I can clearly see how archaic, patriarchal and, above all, unrealistic Eissler's views were. Psychoanalysis may have worked well as a method of analyzing texts, but it wasn't doing its job as therapy. We spent fruitless hours trying to discover why David and I fought, for instance. Eissler didn't have a clue and neither did I. Once he speculated that I pictured myself wafting over a field of penises picking the most appealing. If anything, this was his fantasy, not mine, and it certainly had nothing to do with the problems I was having in relating to another human being.

In a sequel to the suicide story, I wrote about me and David fighting in bed. It was called "Not to Me" and was about how trouble starts when something is very important to one person and a different thing is equally important to the other. A therapist who worked more with relationships than drives would have noticed this in the story and talked to me about it. Would have noted, among other things, how my mother wasn't a very good model for communication skills and I had a lot to learn.

Eissler, though he felt strongly about things like my taking a bath every day—when I told him I didn't, he couldn't suppress his shock that I wasn't even cleansing my private parts—didn't give me any useful pointers about how you talk things over with someone. Perhaps he couldn't. Besides admitting to bad judgment about people, he was exceedingly shy and awkward. (Much later, I heard from a psychologist friend who knew Eissler that he came from a family that was almost as troubled as mine.) Eissler also didn't like the story. In my sessions, he began to suggest that being an academic instead of a fiction writer would provide more play for my ambitions.

Although I was still determined to be a writer, I was fascinated by Eissler's method of reading literature and was also beginning to read in psychoanalytic terms. By the time I was a senior at Barnard, I had the feeling that the standard New Critical approach wasn't getting at the heart of things. I thought I could get to a deeper truth by analyzing the emotional meanings. Eissler became a mentor, as we took turns in my hours talking about Yeats's imagery and Hamlet's increasing insight.

It was satisfyingly soothing to analyze texts. It was much easier to track images through texts and find patterns than it was to find meaning in my own puzzling life. Yeats's haunting images distracted me from my ongoing fights with Mother and, since I had finally given David back his ring, my lack of a man. Why did Yeats talk about blood on the ancestral stair, I asked in papers coyly titled "Functions of Imagery 1," "2," and "3." Why did his moon shining down aloof and unperturbable give me shivers up the spine? What were his secrets?

"Yeats has snakes whispering things," I told Eissler excitedly while lying on his nubbly couch, "probably something incestuous."

"Mmm," was all he said, but I could sense him leaning forward with a satisfied expression.

I applied to graduate school only because Miss Colie recommended me for a Woodrow Wilson Fellowship. Because of my upbringing, I didn't think of graduate school as a path to a future profession; I simply wanted an excuse to keep on probing writers' secrets.

"If I go to Columbia, I'm going to write about madness in Yeats," I told Eissler. "Madness, dreaming, and the fool." I identified with Yeats's fool in his cock-eyed cap and bells: inept, awkward, even crazy, but miraculously able to say wise things.

In June of 1958, I graduated from Barnard and, though I hadn't gotten the fellowship, in the fall I started at Columbia. Since I was single now, Eissler thought it would be good for me to learn to masturbate to orgasm. Freud himself thought that clitoral orgasms were something that had to be given up in favor of the truly mature vaginal orgasm, and his disciple Princess Bonaparte went so far as to consider a clitoridectomy. On the other hand, a failure to orgasm led to the damming up of sexual energy, which, according to orthodox theory, increased anxiety and was itself a sign of illness.

Eissler, like Freud, was fascinated by female orgasms, though he probably knew just as little about them. He later wrote an article distinguishing between an aggressive female orgasm characterized by a sharp peak and screams—which he interpreted as a sort of battle cry—and a more male-friendly orgasm characterized by a gentle, wavelike sensation. In any case, not being able to have an orgasm meant you might be caught back in some regressive place where you were fixated on your mouth, say, and spent your free time smoking cigars instead of having good healthy sex. As early as the 1930s a committed Freudian like Helene Deutsch timidly pointed out that many highly functioning wives and mothers were not orgasmic. But the fact, discovered by Phyllis Greenacre, that even psychotics on back wards can have multiple orgasms hadn't yet seriously disturbed analysis's cheerful equation of genital proficiency and mental health.

I was doing pretty well at my masturbation practice when I met a very nice boy named Bruce, a lanky blond who loved Mozart. I wasn't attracted to him in particular, but I was intrigued by a friend he kept talking about, a man named Randy Irons, who, he swore, was a genius and had worked with Einstein at the Institute for Advanced Studies at Princeton.

When I met Randy, I was impressed. Though he was heavyset and had a thick, almost bullish, head, he exuded energy—even his walk was a series of impatient springs forward and his brown eyes had a hypnotic quality. He brought along his girlfriend, Barbara, who was obviously deeply in love with him, but after a few days he called to say they were finished, and we started going out together.

Eissler was almost as excited as I was—a real genius was attracted to me. Eissler saw his main mission as getting me healthy enough to marry. That way I would get the baby that would compensate me for being born without a penis. It was almost too much to hope for that I would find a genius who would compensate me for not being one myself.

After a few dates, Randy took me to meet his friend Lenny Kriegal, a married graduate student at the City College of New York who'd had polio as a child and was just beginning to write his autobiographical stories. Lenny, like Bruce, was convinced of Randy's genius and told me about the advanced courses in physics Randy had taken at Columbia and how he'd bowled over his professors.

After some weeks, Randy invited me to his house and played Beethoven for me. He'd studied piano with Horowitz, he said. But he'd been in a terrible accident and hurt his hands. Now he could only play so-so. I thought his playing was terrific, but after he finished he put on a record of his playing before the "accident" that was even better.

In order to be equal to such a superman, I offered myself to him immediately. To my surprise, sex wasn't so good. Ordinarily that would have bothered Eissler. But he had a theory that fulfilled sexuality and genius were incompatible. During one of my sessions, he told me about a man who came to him with an impotency problem. Eissler thought the man was a Renaissance genius (just as Randy seemed to be) and was afraid if he tampered with his inhibited sexuality he might destroy his genius. Being a therapist, he went ahead: the man's impotence was cured, but he lost his genius.

Pretty soon, Randy began to ask me to lend him money. First just small amounts, then more. He was also clearly still seeing his old girlfriend. He would excuse himself from the table when we were having dinner at a restaurant and call her up.

"Don't worry, baby," I'd hear him saying. "I love you." When we were apart for a few days, he wrote me long flowery letters addressed to "Dearest, passionate truth." It didn't look good.

"A genius isn't bound by the same distinctions as other people," Eissler told me when I complained about Randy's untrustworthy behavior. "Goethe slept with a dagger under his pillow for weeks when he was writing *The Sorrows of Young Werther*. In someone else, that would have been a serious sign of psychosis. In him it was only what he had to do to imagine Werther's character."

Eissler finally got worried when Randy, instead of sending me one of his letters, read it to me over the phone. I never figured out why this was any worse than anything else Randy did, but somehow it convinced Eissler that the man wasn't sincere. He got me to persuade Randy to go to an analyst for an evaluation. The doctor told Eissler that Randy was not analyzable; he would just use insight to manipulate people. Years later, Lenny Kriegal, by then a professor at the City College of New York, wrote about a brilliant impostor who managed to deceive everyone he came in contact with. Of course it was Randy.

As recent books like *Lying on the Couch* have pointed out, analysis is particularly vulnerable to people who lie. All an analyst has to go on is what you choose to say. If you want to play tricks, nothing could be easier.

In a more general way, Eissler couldn't see what was right in front of his face. This was partly because of his temperament—repressed and shy—and the retrograde nature of 1950s culture, but Eissler's skewed vision was also the fault of psychoanalytic theories about women (and drives) and genius. I didn't need to learn to masturbate and find a genius who would give me a baby/penis, I needed some help in getting free of my mother and negotiating everyday life as an independent woman.

Chapter

9

Anatomy is destiny. —SIGMUND FREUD

$\mathcal{I}$t was the summer of 1959, and I persuaded Persia, an Iranian friend from Barnard, to take a trip to France with me. I wanted to get away from analysis for a while and take stock. Unfortunately just before our departure, Persia found out she was pregnant; I became her bridesmaid at a quick wedding at City Hall. Visiting her after the ceremony in her cramped apartment made me want to get away all the more. So when I ran into Jerry Wolker, one day in a bookstore on Morningside Heights, I impulsively invited myself to visit him at his home in Vienna. It was an odd choice for someone who still had nightmares about Nazis, but I felt that with someone there to welcome me, I'd be okay.

Jerry had an appealing dreamy sort of aestheticism. At the party where we had met, he'd impressed me by reciting some lines of Sappho in the original Greek and talking nostalgically about the late Emperor Franz Joseph. I didn't know him well, but he was a reassuring sort of guy, studying international law. He told me that his family had been strongly anti-Nazi during the war. He was in the midst of a love affair that was going badly and I thought we might cheer each other up.

I decided to go to France first, alone, and visit some young artists, friends of Betty Parsons, Mother's dealer. One of them lived in an attic room with a porthole for a window. He was very kind and took me to the museums, the bistros, and even to the flea market to look for an antique chandelier. I ate food I'd never eaten before, snails and brains in butter. And in my red-draped hotel room, I discovered how to masturbate with the water jet of the bidet. It wasn't as much fun as it might have been, though, because I had the feeling that Eissler was lurking, just out of sight, with an approving smile.

I also got dreadfully sick. By the time I reached Jerry in Vienna, I was running a fever and my stomach hurt almost continuously. After trying to eat the tea cakes his mother had prepared to welcome me, I collapsed in a sweat, and Jerry and his mother had to lug me down the narrow stairs and drive me to the Krankenhaus, a grim building on the outskirts of Vienna, surrounded by gnarled trees.

The nurses were nuns in starched hats. They spoke Viennese German and the first word I learned beside *Ja* and *Nein* was *Achtung!* Their guttural tones made me shiver. These were the sounds the Jews had heard ordering them to the gas chambers. When the white-garbed sisters in their neat caps told me briskly to get up or lie down, *essen* or *schlafen,* I imagined them doing the same thing in a concentration camp. I had nightmares in which my mother watched coldly while I was dragged off with the unfit. In real as opposed to dream time, my mother called frequently—panicked angry calls—and tried to get them to send me back home. She was as unnerved by our separation as I was.

I think deep down I experienced my hospital stay as an extended punishment for trying to be independent. It was a slightly more benign version of my childhood nightmares with the doctors as Nazi-like keepers. I was caught, as it were, examined, stripped, and made to wear a humiliating striped gown.

The doctors who wandered in and out of my room were openly intrigued by the fact I was Jewish. Dr. Boehm, the doctor in charge of me, a slim, black-haired man, said bluntly that the Jews had been to blame for what happened to them.

"They wouldn't work with their hands," he said darkly. "They took all the best jobs."

I was naïve enough to wonder if this was true.

"You're different," Boehm added when he saw the look of alarm on my face, "a very nice girl." That didn't make me feel any better. I wondered if Jews as a whole had hidden nasty qualities—just as I did under my nice-girl facade—that made other people hate and want to destroy us.

Thinking about this later, I see that growing up while the Nazis were exterminating Jews created a permanent reservoir of images that coincided with my own fears that I was bad and stupid, selfish, and spoiled, and, above all, deserved to be punished. In a more confident person, unjustified slaughter of one's people would have had a different effect. Jerry, on the other hand, had enough healthy self-esteem to be indignant that the Austrians were still blamed for the Holocaust. "The Jews want to corner the market on suffering," he said, "but other people suffer too." His family had been against Hitler. Jerry's conscience was clear.

I made friends with the only Jewish doctor there, Doctor Armin Reichman, a large gentle man without a mean bone in him. I confided in him, telling him about my affair with Randy and the way I had invited myself to Vienna to escape.

"You don't need someone to sleep with," he told me, sitting on the side of my bed. "You need someone to talk to you." That made sense. I was beginning to tire of Jerry's self-pity and his nostalgic monologues about the emperor and pre-war Vienna.

One day, I heard the head doctor, who had been a prominent Nazi, call Armin *Reichschwein.*"

"How can you let him do that?" I asked him.

"He's just joking," Armin said. "The others do it too. They're just a bunch of jokers." The head doctor had a big thick dueling scar across the right side of his face, and the day after I had heard him call Armin *Reichschwein* he made me lie back over the bed to give me a vaginal examination.

"To see if you are pregnant," he said coarsely. "We don't want to do an appendectomy on you if you are carrying a child."

It is almost impossible to maintain dignity while you are bent over backwards with your legs spread and someone in a white coat is looming over you. "But I'm not pregnant," I said, while his fingers pressed and pushed inside of me. Would they have made the same assumption if I was a nice Austrian girl?

I was there for several weeks while they waited for my colitis to quiet down, reading Rilke and writing poems about black swans, before they whisked me off to the operating room and took out my appendix. When I woke up, Boehm brought it in in a bottle to show me, "before I throw it away," he said. It was all wrinkled and whitish. For a moment I felt relieved, as though all my badness had been concentrated in this rotten bit of flesh. Now that it had been surgically removed, maybe life would be different for me.

But as soon as I got out of the hospital and went to Jerry's house to recuperate, I saw that nothing had changed. Jerry's mother clearly wondered why her wonderful son had brought home this ailing, alien waif. Every morning she gave me reproachful glances while she stoked the beautifully enameled pot-bellied stove in my room.

"My mother thinks you have good qualities," Jerry told me, "but all in the wrong order. All jumbled up." My worst flaws in her opinion were not knowing German and not knowing how to waltz. Jerry was a magnificent dancer and had been chosen to dance the opening waltz at the yearly Viennese Ball. My not knowing how to waltz—despite my hundred lessons—seemed like a deliberate affront not just to Jerry and his mother but to Vienna itself, with its Ringstrasse and Sacher torte and debutantes in white gowns.

I fell back on sex. One night after my scar stopped hurting so much, I went to Jerry's room and summoned him to my bed. For an exhilarating second I was "his queen, his vision in white."

"I thought you were still a *Mädchen,* a maiden," he whispered to me as we were making love. For answer, I bit his lip. I wasn't enjoying this at all. I was afraid the pressure would make my scar open and my guts spill out. Or at the very least, blood would leak between the sutures.

"We'll do it very neatly," the Nazi surgeon had said with his characteristic leer. "That way you can wear a bikini. You'll like that, won't you? Right here," and he ran his finger slowly over my abdomen.

At a crucial moment, Jerry stopped moving and held his breath. Feet were moving slowly down the hall outside the bedroom. "*O Gott, mein Vati,*" Jerry whispered in an agony of fear. "Shh"—he put his hand over my mouth. The footsteps paused for a moment and I imagined Jerry's father's hand reaching out for the knob. I guess he thought better of it.

"You won't force me to marry? Will you?" Jerry stammered when the footsteps had retreated. "Just because my father knows I was with you?"

"Don't worry," I said, blushing more for him than for myself.

I arrived back in New York to begin my second year at Columbia, minus my appendix and with my self-esteem at an all-time low. One day Dick Goldman, a bird-watching millionaire who was an old family friend and also my trustee, called to say he had met just the man for me. His name was Richard Webster and he taught Sanskrit—actually it turned out to be Italian history—at Columbia. The main thing that was right about him, I gathered from Dick's comments, was his class. He wasn't lower middle class like my previous boyfriends, but upper middle, maybe even upper upper middle—a fact that also made Eissler happy. Besides, he was almost family. Richard's mother, Ida, had dated my father when he was a Harvard Law student and she was studying architecture at MIT. Our parents saw each other socially. Ida's condolence letter after my father's death was in the pile my mother kept in her bedroom closet.

Richard invited me to have sherry with him at the Faculty Club with such formal seriousness that he sounded like a character from Trollope. With lingering adolescent provocativeness, I decided that I'd wear my tight blue skirt with black tights and dusted my face with a pale powder that I thought made me look like a decadent poet.

Richard didn't comment on my outfit, though I noticed his strange yellow eyes followed the curve of my skirt intently before looking into my face. He was handsomer than I'd expected, with stern Roman features, and wore a conservative suit and vest with a watch chain like my father's. He held himself in a sort of taut suspense. His speech was measured and formal. He spoke in complete sentences with subclauses.

I'd expected to laugh but found myself fascinated. His interest in me was all the more flattering because he was so guarded. It was also a relief that he was so self-contained. I was tired of other people's emotions washing over me.

We started going out, mostly to the theater. When he took me home from a matinee of *A Raisin in the Sun*—a play about a black family—he stayed to dinner and listened politely to Mother talk about painting a black epic and her work in the Urban League. My father had been a director of the League, and now she was a director, too, and was thinking of writing a book about integration. The whole thing annoyed me. I hated seeing her on television, where she appeared several times in her capacity as director—an elegant white woman who sent her children to a posh private school—to talk about the beauties of integration to a middle class that was getting it forced down their throats. But Richard was impressed.

"Your mother is quite a lady," he told me after dinner. He was very critical of his own parents and clearly thought that Mother had deeper, better, values.

Richard at thirty-one still lived with his parents in a beautiful old building on Sixty-third Street off Madison Avenue. His mother had designed the interior of the apartment herself. It had a huge living room divided into two seating areas with recessed lighting and a discreet bar. One of the sofas was covered in gorgeous orange silk. There were off-white Peruvian rugs, Impressionist paintings, and a Calder mobile. The bookshelves were filled with leather-bound sets of Rossetti and Dickens. The apartment had an ordered calm that relaxed me and made me feel safe. I even liked the formal dining room with its family portraits.

Richard's mother, Ida, was a tiny woman, under five feet, but bursting with the energy that made her the first woman to graduate from MIT's architecture school. She had straw-blond hair and pale eyes. When I visited the first time, she immediately brought up my father. It was clear that whatever had happened between them, she still thought about it with a certain charge of excitement.

"I think I was the only girl Wolf went out with who didn't sleep with him," she told me. "We used to play cards in his room every week. Once some of the fellows came over when I was there and I hid in the closet. Because they wouldn't have believed, you know, that it was innocent. When I started going out with Richard's father, he made me stop going." She sighed.

"I wish your mother would shorten her skirts and not wear those capes and fur boots," she said on another occasion. "They make her look like a Cossack."

"Ida pretends to love your mother," Richard commented later, "but she really hates her. She can't see why your father married such an eccentric." He looked pleased. It didn't take me long to figure out he had an adversarial relationship with his parents.

The Websters tended to be judgmental about people who weren't *comme il faut*. Assimilated Jews like my family, they had sanitized their name from something like Gertner to Webster—chosen because when the family arrived in this country in the previous century, it looked as though Daniel Webster might be president. Richard's maternal grandfather had become mayor of Cedarhurst, Long Island, and had a statue erected to him. This was about as far away from being Jewish as you could get, and the Websters wanted to keep it that way. Their tolerance for individual differences was minimal. The women wore pearls and had their skirts the proper length. The men went to the office, made lots of money, drank martinis at cocktail hour, and played tennis at the club on weekends. Even though Ida was quite a maverick, with her high-powered career—she had fifty men working under her—she dressed and acted like an old-fashioned wife, giving her paycheck over to her husband with a kiss and letting him dole out the money as if he'd made it. Richard was scornful of her "cult of possessions" and of the way both his parents measured success.

"I wasn't at all the son they wanted," Richard explained. "I was a bookish child, no good at sports. One day my father got so exasperated at my inability to hit a tennis ball that he threw the racket at my head."

I nodded sympathetically. I'd had my own troubles with tennis. Richard's father Morton—a stockbroker specializing in arbitrage—looked so mild, it was hard to imagine him having fits of temper. But once when he was reading the paper and Ida was trying to talk to him, he lowered it for a second and asked her dryly if she really thought she could compete with the *New York Times*. I gathered from Richard that Ida had worn Morton down over the years. His happiest time had been when he was a pilot during the war. Next to the wet bar hung a photo of him looking handsome in his pilot's uniform.

Like Grandma's family, the Oppenheimers, the Websters thought being a professor was a second-rate profession. "They wanted me to go into business," Richard told me dryly, "or at least get a job at Harvard. No, I was a disappointment. My sister was the ideal child. She married a CEO."

"My milk was too rich for him," Ida told me once, when she saw me looking at a photo of Richard in his pram looking rather stoically ahead of him. "It was like cream. Dick threw it up. I had to feed him condensed milk. He couldn't chew properly either. Until he was three he drank mashed food from a bottle." I was enough of a Freudian by now to be sure Ida had a bad attitude towards mothering. Unlike my mother she admitted that she hated being away from her work.

"I wasn't cut out to be a mother," she told me later. Her first baby, a boy, had been stillborn. She was probably still mourning when she had Richard. But I had no sympathy for her. My sympathy was all for Richard as a baby not getting good milk, as a sensitive little boy in white shorts being bullied by his father to conform. His family didn't value him. No wonder he was sarcastic to his mother when she spoke to him, appeared ungrateful when she did little things for him like pack his suitcase or wash his socks. He had been neglected and misunderstood by his mother just the way I had. Our anger at the way we'd been treated drew us together. I decided early on that I would understand him. It never occurred to me that I might not be up to repairing the damage that had been done.

The first time we slept together, Richard asked me to marry him. Mother had taken a short trip, leaving me alone in the house.

"I'm engaged," I told her when she came home.

"I should never have left. I knew it," she cried, almost in a frenzy. "I should never have let Dr. Kris persuade me to go."

I was triumphant. Somehow, I'd made a stand. Done something she couldn't approve or absorb.

"He reminds me of a man I was in love with once," Mother said one night after Richard went home, "Mortimer Adler. A brain on a toothpick."

"I thought Richard reminded you of your father?" I said, annoyed at her meanness and the fact that Mortimer Adler was another episode in her life I knew nothing about.

"Him too," she said enigmatically. She had a tendency, I realized later, to absorb events in my life into hers as though my life were a mediocre replay.

I told Weasal what Mother said about Richard's being a brain on a toothpick.

"Your mother's found her match, that's all," Weasal shook her head sagely. "She won't be wrapping this man around her little finger. You won't be either. He knows how to handle the both of you." I agreed with her. I didn't like the way my affairs were getting briefer and closer together. I had the feeling I might be turning into the whore my father was always worrying about. Besides, until

Jerry had turned the tables on me, I had treated men badly. Collecting their pins and watches and rings the way a headhunter does his shrunken heads. I had the feeling that I needed to be taken in hand. And Richard seemed to be the man to do it.

"This is God's house," Richard announced solemnly one day as we were passing the Fifth Avenue synagogue that his grandfather was affiliated with. I couldn't believe he was serious. But he was. When I laughed, he leaned over and lightly boxed my ear. "It's not a joke." I flinched, but I was secretly thrilled at his intensity. Later he explained that he was studying Hebrew and reading the Torah and the Rabbinic commentaries with a distinguished tutor, much to his parents' dismay. His study and observance weren't, I suspect, because he believed in God, but because he wanted to show his solidarity with Jewish tradition and the Jewish people.

"Religion may not be the healthiest solution," Dr. Eissler said, echoing Freud's view that belief in God is a manifestation of childish yearning. As usual he picked the wrong sign of neurosis. He didn't comment on my boxed ear.

Oddly enough, Richard's Judaism was attractive to me. I liked it that, rejecting materialism and social functions, business and tennis, he believed in something. I had been taught to be scornful of religion, but secretly I yearned for meaning with a capital *M*. And there was something touching in Richard's view, exemplified by a joke he told me: One Torah student asks the other, "Did you see the man in the back row davening?" "You mean the one with the humped back and the limp? The one with the blind eye?" "Yes, that one. A beautiful Jew. A *shayne* Yid." It wasn't appearances that mattered. It was the spirit.

I had taken class as the battling ground with my father. Richard had taken up religion in the face of disapproval from both his parents. That in itself made a bond between us. We were goading our parents in their most sensitive spots. His mother would become almost apoplectic when Richard mentioned some news item about the ultra-Orthodox Hasidim. "Why can't they wake up and live in this century," she would say, scrunching up her face in disgust. "Those ear curls, the black coats—they should have stayed in Poland." Sometimes she even hinted to me that she hoped I would wean him away from all this foolishness. She was afraid he would pick up and leave for Israel and never come back.

I nodded politely but secretly sided with him. Vienna had given me a new sense of vulnerability. It seemed brave to take on an identity that was so hated and despised. Richard was slender and blond, and had an English name. He didn't have to insist on his Jewishness, but he did. He said people who denied their origins cut away part of themselves, became shallow. For someone struggling as I was with self-hatred, that sounded right.

What bothered me about Richard wasn't his religion. It was the way he touched me, awkwardly as though he felt squeamish. "He won't open his mouth when he kisses me," I complained to Eissler, "he clamps his teeth shut."

This didn't bother Eissler.

"He's very shy," Eissler told me. "This may be the first time he has been in love. You must be patient." He studied the passport photo Richard had given me. Long face, full lips, wavy blond hair. "A real intellectual," he said with satisfaction. "Probably you'll never find anyone so compatible again."

At another session, I complained that Richard didn't want to go to a poetry reading I was giving with Judy Johnson at The First Born Coffee House.

"You have to remember," Eissler said, "that the man is the one who earns a living. His is the primary profession. Besides, he came to one reading already, didn't he?" Eissler asked, in a tone that implied Richard's generosity.

"Yes, he came . . ."

"And even brought his friends." That was true too. He had brought Peter Gay—the historian who later wrote a biography of Freud—and his wife, Ruthie.

I had chanted my poems, wearing black of course, and beating on the table with the palm of my hand:

> Is this the face of God, I cried,
> Is this the lamb, the one who died?

"So much *schmerz*," Peter Gay commented to Richard after the reading. "Your girlfriend must have unpleasant dreams." My mother's friends were more enthusiastic. Betty Parsons and José Guerrero both came up and put their arms around me. "Wonderful," Betty said in her throaty voice.

Mother was jealous. "Next time don't invite them," she said. "They're my friends. Leave them alone."

Richard was researching a book about the Fascists and the Church, and asked me to come with him to Italy that summer. Eissler thought this would give me an opportunity to see whether I could adjust to being a scholar's wife. We lived in a *pensione* in central Florence run by two wrinkled sisters named Bandelli. It was very beautiful, with a columned loggia that ran all around the outside and big rooms with high ceilings. Every day, Richard went off to work in the archives and I sat in the *pensione,* too upset by the July heat to go anywhere. When I poked my head out, I felt as though I'd melt. Inside it was dark and cool and I lay on my bed like a woman in a harem and waited, bored and sorry for myself, for him to come back for lunch. The heat didn't bother him at all. He ate huge plates of pasta, the oil glistening on his chin, then took me to bed.

When Eissler heard that Richard made love six times in one broiling Italian afternoon, he was triumphant. "Here you have a man who really wants to make love to a woman."

When we went back to Florence again the next year, I thought I'd bring my own work, so I'd have something to do. I'd started writing a novel about my trip to Vienna. Since I was entering a new phase of life, I wanted to make Richard a present of my past. Sort of wrap the whole thing up and start again.

Richard read bits of it over my shoulder when he came back from the library. "More of your unpleasant fantasies," he said. What hurt me was that he didn't see how all the pain was tending toward something good. But I wasn't angry, though in retrospect I should have been. Instead I worried that he was right. That maybe I did have a diseased imagination: I pretended to be horrified by the Nazi surgeon, but scenes of torture physically excited me. Secretly, I imagined people tied to stakes and whipped. It was awful, and somehow Richard, with his yellow cat eyes, could see it written on my heart. He saw it, but he didn't back off.

Despite Richard's criticism, I found a New York agent when we got back. Toni Strassman had known and admired my father and had worked at Viking for many years. She was enthusiastic about the book and immediately started sending it out. Publishers were respectful but reluctant. Editors were mystified by my sort of meditative circling with neither a happy nor a tragic ending.

"Reality is more interesting than fantasy anyway," Richard said, then smiled. In the fall he would start a new job at the University of California at Berkeley, and he wanted me to marry him and come to California with him. "It's the land of milk and honey, you know." I think it was the biblical allusion that finally got me.

When I told my mother I'd decided to get married and join Richard out west, she headed straight for her bedroom window. The bars had been removed several years back.

"I can't stand it," she screamed, opening the window. A blast of cold wet air streamed in. It was raining.

"What are you doing?" I screamed back, knowing perfectly well. She put her knee up on the radiator cover and began crawling out onto the sill. I grabbed her arm with a strength I didn't think I had and pulled. She toppled back against me, into the room. I was going to hug her and try to soothe her, but before I could do anything, she reached out and clawed me on the neck, hissing like a cornered cat. She wouldn't stop struggling. Finally, not able to think of what else to do, I slapped her hard in the face. She went dead still and stared at me, her eyes burning. I wanted to kill her.

"Damn you," I could have said, "you bitch—what do you think you're doing? How many times does this have to happen?" But I couldn't even open my mouth.

I dragged her over to her bed and pushed her down against the pillows, where she lay sobbing. I kept a hand on her shoulder while I dialed Dr. Kris. "Here," I said after I'd told Dr. Kris what happened. "Here, listen, it'll make you feel calmer," and I jammed the receiver, not too gently, against her ear. She listened for a few minutes, sniffling and sobbing. Then she started to explain: she'd just been overcome by panic, didn't really mean it, just felt so frightened at being left. If I'd been watching a movie with a scene like this, I'd probably have started feeling sorry for her. But I couldn't. I just felt violent stomach cramps.

Later, thinking about it, I was angry at Dr. Kris, too, for not doing her job better. Why did she accept all these rationalizations? What good did so much acceptance of bad behavior do anyone? It didn't make Mother less prone to flamboyant gestures. If anything, I thought it made her more self-indulgent. To my mind there should have been a rule. No more death threats, for any reason, period, or the analysis ends. The truth was, Dr. Kris was being emotionally blackmailed. In the end, she was more chicken than I was. Everything had a reason. No blame. No motive for change.

Ida didn't trust my mother to plan the wedding, so she did it, booked a ballroom at the Ritz, hired the caterers, made up the menu, sent out invitations. All we had to do was receive the gifts. Crystal and silver started pouring in. Ida was ecstatic.

"I love the idea of your going with Dick," she told me.

All the preparations had a negative effect on me. I'd hated the only big wedding I'd ever been to. I didn't want all this glass and all these tea sets. I hadn't the slightest inclination to keep house.

"I can't go through with it," I told Richard. "I'm terribly sorry. I'll come out after a few months and live with you, but I just can't get married, not yet."

"Why not?"

"I'm afraid, afraid you'll change." Turn into a monster, was what I was thinking. I didn't know how it would happen, but somehow it would. I probably felt I deserved it for being such a bad daughter.

My mother didn't say a word, but she sent back all the engagement presents. Ida was distraught. "I don't think you should live together out there if you're not married," she said. "It might hurt Dickie's reputation."

"All right," I told her, "I'll get an apartment, for the sake of appearances. But I won't live there."

I didn't want to go out West right away because I was finishing up the final revisions of my master's thesis on Yeats. I also had the illusion that I could come to a sense of closure in my therapy. I hadn't gained much insight into my problems. I still fought with my mother and had attacks of anxiety. But I was going to miss Eissler nonetheless. He had been both surrogate father and mentor to me for four years, since I was nineteen.

Eissler, on his side, felt it was an achievement to have gotten me in good enough shape to marry. He was particularly happy that I was able to have an orgasm, not only by myself but with my chosen husband in the superior position. He felt that allowing myself to be symbolically mastered was a sign of the depth of my love. Otherwise, he was guardedly optimistic. He hoped I would feel much better outside my mother's orbit.

Eissler warned me when Richard went off to begin his job at Berkeley that he wouldn't do well by himself, wouldn't tolerate being alone. When I visited him, I saw that was true. He'd rented a house from a professor who was away on sabbatical. The place was a mess.

"I spent all morning on my knees scrubbing the bathroom floor," I told Eissler proudly when I came back. "It was covered with ants! First I poured boiling water on them."

"Are you really going to marry this man?" Eissler grimly asked me. "He's very neurotic."

"Oh no, you can't turn around like this on me. For over a year you've been trying to persuade me to let myself go, to commit myself, and now you change your mind and tell me the opposite? Well, I won't change mine." I was flushed from my victory over the ants. Things were easy if you just took charge.

"He might leave you alone a lot. Retreat into his study and close the door. Are you prepared for that?"

"He's a scholar," I said ingenuously. Something was clearly bothering Eissler, but he wouldn't tell me straight out what it was.

Eissler's worry, when it finally came out, was triggered by what he saw as a sexual problem. I had mentioned that Richard got up several times a night to pee. Eissler was very worried by this. He thought this meant Richard had to keep checking to see if his thing was still there, that he had some basic sexual insecurity. A urologist told Richard that he had a urinary problem; eventually he might need an operation, but he could wait until after he'd had children. Eissler wasn't satisfied. He got me to persuade Richard to see a shrink named Merton Gill in California.

"The shrink told Richard that if he got analyzed he might not want to marry me," I relayed to Eissler, "so he's not going back." The logic seemed clear to me, but Eissler didn't seem happy about it.

It didn't occur to me to wonder what the other shrink had told Eissler.

When I was in Berkeley, visiting Richard's office, he pulled a letter out of his desk and handed it to me. I recognized Eissler's handwriting on the envelope. The letter—as formal a letter as Richard would have written himself—asked him to delay his marriage to me. I was shocked. Eissler had said Richard was neurotic, but so what? I was too. That was no reason to try and stop our marriage. It's not that there wasn't a precedent for this sort of analytic meddling. Freud had interfered actively in his patients' lives, even telling them whom to marry and whether they could get divorced. But it certainly wasn't acceptable practice in America in the 1950s.

"This is so unprofessional," Richard said. "The man's clearly in love with you." I was childish enough to be pleased by the idea. I was also too embarrassed to mention the letter to Eissler—as if I'd caught him doing something he shouldn't. At any rate I didn't take his warning seriously, and gradually it faded from my mind. I had made up my mind to make this marriage work and I didn't really want to know anything that might stop me.

Chapter

10

~

Apart from ridicule, the counterrevolutionary
period never employed a more withering or
destructive weapon against feminist insurgence
than the Freudian accusation of penis envy.
                                        —KATE MILLETT

A month later I was out in California, enrolled in graduate school. In some ways Berkeley was an escape—from my mother, from Park Avenue, and from a whole world of young women who flashed their diamonds, wore mink jackets and walked white poodles. The Berkeley flatlands stretching from the bay to the campus were undistinguished, but once you rose into the hills it was a different story. The hills rose steeply, giving breathtaking views from every curve as they circled higher until they reached Tilden Park, running along the ridge, crisscrossed with fifty miles of trails. The perfect setting for freedom.

Richard's house was in the Berkeley hills on the south side of campus. Although the house was small and depressingly underfurnished, it had a terrace that hung out over space under a brilliant sky and was surrounded by evergreen trees. I sat on the terrace just hugging my knees and breathing the good air. Richard took me down into town for Chinese food at the Yen Ching and to my first service ever, at the Conservative synagogue, Beth Israel, on Bancroft. For Richard, too, Berkeley represented a dreamland away from his parents' materialism and their critical eye. A permission to be as Jewish as he liked. To me the Jewish service was as exotic as the Chinese meal.

Before I left New York for Berkeley, Eissler had arranged for me to be transferred to another analyst, a friend of his and Anna

Freud's, another old-guard Freudian, Anna Maenchen. She hadn't been able to find a time to see Eissler about me, she told me, she'd been so busy at the annual meeting of the American Psychoanalytic Association. But he persisted, arriving at her hotel at one in the morning. I could imagine Eissler rushing across the city in the dead of night, intent on my salvation.

Anna Maenchen—her nickname was Anya—seemed like a more practical person. She was short, with an intelligent face rimmed by graying curls and a certain briskness heightened by her German accent. She lived in the North Berkeley hills, in a house on the edge of Greenwood Common, an enclosed community space with flowering cherry trees and a grassy center where children could play safely. I took that space as a hopeful emblem—like the Winnicottian safety zone where a child, playing, begins to separate from its mother. There was a magnificent view in the room Maenchen used as an office, straight through windowed pines to the Golden Gate Bridge. This too was hopeful and for a while at the beginning I had a recurring dream of looking out a window at the ocean, a wide expansive view.

But more often than not, Maenchen drew the curtain to keep the sun from bleaching her rugs. Certainly she drew one metaphorically. I never felt safe there and rarely felt as though my view was expanding.

If Eissler hoped that Maenchen would lead me to some quick insights that would keep me from marrying Richard, it didn't work that way. I told her about my doubts, about Eissler's surprising change of mind, but she said very little. She wanted to know what I felt. Maenchen subscribed to Freud's theory that having a baby is woman's way of compensating for her penisless state. I suppose it was to test my readiness for this developmental step that she placed a small male figure made of wood on her desk in front of me at an early session. Next to it, inches from my nose, was a photo of a handsome young man.

"Is this your son?" I asked her timidly.

"Yes," she answered with obvious pride. "He's a physicist."

I was impressed. Not only did she have this beautiful office, but she had a good-looking, successful son. Without thinking, I picked up the wooden figure, the kind artists use to learn anatomy, and started to bend its arms and legs. I made it sit, then lie curled on its side. It kept me from feeling nervous.

"Do you want a child?" Maenchen asked, looking at me intently.

"I hadn't thought about it," I said.

"I think you have," she said. And of course by now I had.

Richard hadn't turned into a monster at all. When I came home in the late afternoon after I finished my classes, his eyes followed me around the room.

"You make me happy," he told me in one of his rare statements of emotion. I was glad. It didn't seem hard. Richard couldn't do anything practical. He couldn't drive a car, for instance, or cook, or pack a suitcase, so anything I did was an improvement. I bought a Chinese lantern to hang over the bare lightbulb in our living room, delighted with my initiative as if I'd decorated a whole house from scratch.

Next, I got a cookbook and tried to teach myself to cook. He ate my burnt toast and crumbling meatballs without a murmur. When he asked me if I would keep kosher and I said no, he accepted it in good grace. He even suggested we take company out to the Faculty Club for dinner until I felt comfortable. Since both of us were abysmal housekeepers, we got a woman to come in a couple of times a week to clean. But I was afraid marriage would change things. Whenever I thought about it, I cried.

"Marry me," he kept saying. "You'll feel better. How long are you going to keep me waiting? It's bad for both of us." He was afraid that at the end I'd change my mind and go back to New York. But who would have been crazy enough to do that?

When I told Maenchen we were getting married, she nodded sagely. She'd known we would, she said. In spite of my doubts, I don't remember ever discussing alternatives—like staying by myself for a while, seeing what it was like living alone. I think after watching my mother with Dr. Kris, I expected some practical guidance. Dr. Kris was always giving concrete suggestions. But Maenchen didn't ask me what I expected or wanted from my marriage. Or even why—aside from Eissler's mysterious forebodings—I thought Richard might turn into someone who hated me. She just listened, as most orthodox analysts would have done.

I had a wedding dress made for me, a copy of a Bavarian dress I had bought in Vienna with Jerry. It was white and had a tight bodice with hooks up the front, and white velvet trim. Richard bought me an orchid. He asked a friend in the English Department, Norman Rabkin, to be our witness, and on March 3, 1961, we drove to City Hall in Norman's Volkswagen Bug and were married by a black judge.

"I hope you don't take this lightly," the judge told us after Richard had put the ring on my finger, "just because there is no big ceremony. Marriage is a serious thing."

Our bedroom was half underground like a cave; you looked out into tangled roots and bushes. My wedding ring was a simple gold band, with LOVE, R and the date in Hebrew. Richard had refused to get me an engagement ring, probably to offend his mother's sense of propriety. That first night, the ring seemed to burn on my finger. I had nightmares I hadn't had since childhood. But in the morning, everything was okay. Richard hadn't grown wolf fangs in the night. I was simply married.

After we'd been married a year, Richard took me to a fancy restaurant in San Francisco and ordered champagne. It hasn't been so bad, has it? he asked me. No, I said, it's been wonderful. And I meant it.

A few weeks later, a friend in graduate school, Ann Belsey, a slim, pert, competitive blonde, got pregnant.

"Why don't you do it too," she suggested. "It would be fun to be pregnant together."

"How about school?" I'd gotten my master's—UC had made me do it over, their way—and was moving toward my qualifying exams for the doctorate.

She shrugged her slim shoulders. "I'm a little more tired, that's all. When I get nauseous I just nibble on saltines."

It never occurred to me to ask what happens *after* the baby is born.

By then, we were in a small bright three-room house just up the hill from my analyst. It had a big plate-glass window facing the bay and a window box in which I grew pansies with soft funny faces. We had a fat tortoiseshell tabby that Richard carried around and fussed over, giving it bits from his plate.

He made a face when I told him I thought I'd like to get pregnant.

"But I thought we got the cat to see how it would be with a baby," I said, trying to make him smile.

"No, we got a cat because I like cats," he said, dead serious. "I don't much like babies. In fact I don't like them at all, but if you insist on having one, it's all right—as long as you take care of it." Married women had a right to have children, he told me grimly. It amazes me now that I never questioned him about his feelings. I just went blithely ahead, assuming that he'd love our baby when it came.

I was supposed to be in analysis now, lying on the couch with Maenchen at her post behind me. She didn't make any attempt to get me to think about what might happen to our marriage if my husband really meant what he said about babies. She was still busy trying to get me to understand my competition with my brother and my penis envy. She went to great lengths with her symbolic interpretations. If I came into the office with a walking stick or a branch I'd picked up on the way over, she'd accuse me of fondling an imaginary penis. This was maddening, but I didn't know how to fight back, to explain that sure I was jealous of my brother, and sure I noticed all the attention he got because of his little thing. But that didn't mean I still wanted one.

If anyone really wanted male power, it was probably Maenchen. She once told me how she climbed a mountain in Switzerland all by herself in a raging storm, worrying her husband. She had balls at least. I think it annoyed her that I was a wimp. In retrospect, her theories and her gut feelings seem contradictory.

"You are not really an aggressive person," she once told me when I had expressed envy of a friend whose career was taking off. "Not very ambitious either. But you should be glad. Many ambitious women are unable to have an orgasm."

She wasn't exactly hostile to my work but she kept questioning my need to do it, just as Eissler had. Do you really want to be an intellectual? she would ask me. Couldn't you be just as happy working in the garden? There are some housewives who are truly contented, you know—and so on.

I'd read enough theory to know that overuse of the brain in a woman could be a form of penis envy. Envy was one of the things Maenchen stressed. Unlike Eissler, who often attributed better motives to me than I really had, she saw me as envious not only of my brother but of my glamorous mother. Eissler went out of his way to give generous interpretations of his patients' behavior: once he even defended a woman who had murdered her children; his argument was that she was trying to spare them suffering. Maenchen erred the other way, looking at whatever I did in the worst possible light. If I offered my brother a piece of toast, she would suggest that I secretly wanted him to choke. On the other hand, she never criticized Richard. He was the reality I had to adjust to.

I got pregnant immediately. When three months were almost up, I started to bleed. Richard took me to the hospital, blood flowing down the front of my nightgown. "I was afraid you were going to die," he told me the next morning, voice trembling. "I walked in the park until dawn."

I may have thought I was going to die too, the hemorrhage was so severe. Afterward, I lay on the couch next to our flower box and wept, sure my college abortion had made it impossible for me to have children.

Richard brought me tea and toast and tucked Grandma's afghan around my feet, almost pathetically grateful that I was still around. But when I told him I wanted to get pregnant again as soon as the doctor told me I could, he blanched.

"Why?" he asked me, quoting the Bible: "Aren't I as much to you as seven sons?"

"It's not the same," I said. I had conceived the first time as a sort of whim, but now having a baby became a challenge—it was the only thing I wanted. There was an undertone of fear in it, too. I needed to prove that I hadn't damaged myself, that I was a fully functioning woman. I think I must have hurt Richard, made him feel that he wasn't enough for me. When I did get pregnant again, he was sullen, afraid I was going to miscarry and ruin his research year in Italy. He had gotten a big grant in 1962 and the university had given him time off at half pay to work on his new book.

Maenchen seemed to suspect I miscarried for some emotional reason—perhaps some hostility towards my unborn child. She found me a gynecologist with an analytic background who spoke to me in a low soothing voice as though he thought I was about to slit my wrists. I fired him and got a doctor who treated me like a normal person. But meanwhile Richard was becoming more agitated. He clearly felt that having a baby was going to ruin more than his sab-batical. A little input from Maenchen could have been helpful here. She could have talked to me about the strain having a baby puts on couples. About men's feelings of being left out. About Richard's possible jealousy and fear. About anything real.

Instead she probed so hard to unearth some deep internal reason for miscarrying that I began to wonder about it myself. When I started to bleed again just before we were due to leave on Richard's sabbatical, I worried: What if my badness—noted by Mother al-ready when I was six—was killing my child? What if I thought of him or her as a dangerous sibling, a rival instead of my child—or worse, some sort of parasitic growth, a tumor that had to be eject-ed? Dr. Deutsch, Mother's early analyst, reported fantasies like this in her two-volume *Psychology of Women* and she was always using them to explain miscarriages in her patients. Deutsch herself had trouble keeping a pregnancy going and only succeeded, she thought, because a cherished friend got pregnant at the same time.

With all this in mind, I wasn't going to take any chances. When I noticed that my orgasms triggered contractions, I stopped having them—undoubtedly confirming Richard's worst fears. The voyage over to Italy on the luxury liner *Michelangelo* took place in a mias-ma of anxiety.

Richard had rented an old villa in Florence on Viale Michelange-lo. It was rundown and heated by an erratically performing coal stove, but it had a view from the back of olive trees and white oxen plowing in the fields. I think just getting away from Maenchen did me good. I passed the three-month mark, found the midwife who was going to deliver the baby, and settled down to my life. Richard worked in the archives, and I passed my days buying exquisitely em-broidered baby clothes at a place called La Cicogna—The Stork—and working on a second novel about a man in love with two women: a selfish, sexually predatory bitch and a plainer but creative and nurturing woman who gets pregnant and—unlike me at Swarthmore—decides to have the baby. My first novel was still be-ing shopped around by my agent, Toni. I knew I needed to write to keep sane, but I still didn't think of myself as a writer. It was simply something I did. And since Richard clearly didn't like what I wrote, I kept pretty quiet about it.

Though Richard wasn't happy with my pregnancy, being

pregnant nevertheless seemed like a more legitimate occupation, and I genuinely loved it. Loved getting bigger and bigger. I had maternity clothes made by a seamstress from the richest velvets and brocades I could find, and admired myself in the mirror. Finally I had breasts, round and white and smooth as marble. It didn't bother me that sex with Richard was only lukewarm. I had so much else to think about.

The week before my baby was due, my ankles became swollen and I had to go into the clinic. Too much prosciutto, they told me. I was retaining fluid in a big way. They put a bed in my room and Richard came and slept there. The night before Lisa was born he stayed out until early morning. He looked pale and unhappy when he came back, and told me a confusing story about being at a party. Some sort of switch in my head alerted me not to ask questions. Even if I had asked he would have put me off with, "Oh, just a party, some people I know." He wouldn't have said, "I'm terrified I'm going to lose you. This whole business makes me sick. You lying here with swollen belly, swollen legs, thinking about nothing else but that thing inside you. I don't know what I'm going to do, how I'm going to live with this." For my part, I couldn't have imagined that he was so distressed that he was going to withdraw, even retreat, into places where I couldn't follow him.

My contractions started that afternoon and went on all night. Richard went off to get the midwife at three in the morning and they sat on either side of me, arguing amicably in Italian over which profession—midwife or professor of history—required more sacrifices. Just when they were really getting into it, I threw up. As I was finally wheeled off to the delivery room at about nine-thirty, Richard bent over me. "Remember, keep your eyes open," he whispered. He was afraid if I didn't the nuns might baptize our Jewish baby.

Having a baby was like nothing I could possibly have imagined. I had taken natural childbirth classes—another woman's husband had done the exercises with me since Richard wouldn't participate—so I knew how to relax and pant, and though the pain during the transition phase was much stronger than I'd expected, was able to stay calm. What was amazing was the way my body seemed seized as if by an outside force, lifted up at the hips and then slammed down on the table. The contractions themselves had an organic rhythm. They built up gradually like music and then, just when I thought I was going to scream, they would fade and there'd be a blessed moment of stillness before the next contraction started. If I'd fought the rhythm, I'm sure it would have been hell—I had writhed and cried during my miscarriage—but I let myself go completely. If I started to panic, I'd glance up at the big clock on the wall and assure myself that there were only a few more seconds until I got to the still point. That fraction of a moment's rest was like a drink of cool water.

When the transition was finished, there was less pain. For the first time in my life, I had a sense of my inner anatomy, of the tube of muscle inside me tensing like a fist to propel my baby out. I had an exhilarating sense of strength, as though there was nothing I couldn't do. But after what seemed like a long time pushing, I got frightened—I had been in labor sixteen hours—and asked for the gas mask (*la maschera*). The nurses started smiling and offered me oxygen. Later I found out that they thought I was pleading for my child to be a boy (*un maschio*). When Lisa finally was born they rushed her into the other room, afraid I was going to have hysterics. Finally they announced apologetically, "*Ma signora, e una femina,*" drawing out the last syllable dolefully. The misunderstanding was cleared up and they brought me Lisa.

From the first, Lisa was an exquisite creature. She didn't have the crinkled monkeyish look of newborns. Her skin was smooth as silk, and she had a short fuzz of red-gold hair. When I brought her home, I would stare at her for hours while I lay nursing her, unable to believe that this perfect child was really mine.

At first I was shy with her, as though she were an angel that I was inviting into a modest house. My luck for once seemed too good and it frightened me half to death. I weighed Lisa before and after every feeding to make sure she was getting enough milk. I swaddled her too tightly because I was afraid she'd kick off her covers and catch cold.

Once, when there was a tiny drop of moisture at the tip of her nose and her face looked red, I called my Italian pediatrician in a panic. Finally he got around to asking me how hot it was in the room. I had a heater on full force to keep out the March chill and had wrapped poor Lisa in layers of clothes including a bonnet and blanket. There was an Italian thermometer in the room, but I was so nervous I'd translated it incorrectly. It was nearly eighty degrees. No wonder she was red in the face.

After a while, my nervousness decreased. I stopped running into her room at night listening to see if she was breathing. When the weather got nicer, I took her for long walks up the Viale. She started to smile at me, a wonderful limpid smile of pure happiness. I began to recognize the other mothers and nurses wheeling their prams. We'd exchange greetings. "*O che angelo dal cielo,*" one of them told me, looking under the hood of Lisa's pram.

I tried to get Richard to join in, bathing her or changing her. But partly because I was so inexperienced myself, it went badly. He made the bathwater too hot and she screamed bloody murder. A few months later when I got him to offer her some spoons of applesauce, she spit them out. He threw up his hands and left her to me. Later, I thought, when she could talk, it would be easier.

When things had calmed down a little, my mother came for a visit. I had found her a room in the convent's guest house across the street. When she saw the crucifix in her room and the flies on the lightbulb, she called me in hysterics, and demanded I find her another place. Didn't I know her Catholic nurse had terrified her as a child? And the flies . . . When she saw Lisa, though, she was ecstatic.

"I feel you've given me back a life for the one that was lost," she said, as though she were onstage, but she didn't have the courage to hold my baby. Later, she took me shopping and bought me a coral necklace on the Ponte Vecchio—coral was famous in Italy for warding off the evil eye.

"She is a beautiful baby," Maenchen agreed when I showed her a photo of Lisa at six months, "and healthy too." In the photo Lisa was lying on the grass in front of our brown-shingled house—we'd moved again—and was looking around alertly. Her red-gold fuzz of hair was longer now and she had wide-open brown eyes.

"When I first saw you," Maenchen added musingly, "you looked like such a stray, such a waif. I really didn't know if you would make it."

I flushed with shame. I thought I had looked pretty good. I'd put on a nice circle skirt and my sweater set, combed my hair. I saw myself through her eyes as one of Dickens's orphan children, creeping through the streets with a haunted look on her face.

Maenchen liked to think of herself as an objective, neutral presence. But was this neutrality, describing your patient in the same terms as a mangy dog? I had my doubts, though I couldn't have articulated them then. Instead of dwelling on my infirmities, she might have commented on what I'd done well. Besides caring for my baby, I'd written another novel that my agent loved, and cooked and shopped and cared for my husband. Now when Lisa napped in the afternoon, I studied for my Ph.D. orals. What more did Maenchen want from me? In our sessions, her voice would get thick with irritation—which she would always deny. Or she would cut or fold paper, or fiddle around behind me. Once or twice I caught her snoring.

"I'm not asleep," she would say. "Why do you think that?" But she was.

Two years later, in 1965, when I passed my orals, the head of my committee told me my feminine charm made my faults appear like virtues and, as required, I smiled. Feminism had not hit the English Department. The professors attending my prospectus exam a month later, in which I presented my plan for my dissertation, were similarly middle-aged and male, and even more patronizing. One, with a walrus moustache, pompously inquired why I thought psychology was relevant: wouldn't Madame Blavatsky's theosophical teachings be more pertinent to Yeats than Freud? Another observed that a prized faculty member had already "done" Yeats's plays. What made me think I had anything to add? My project of dealing with Yeats' entire work seemed too ambitious. Why didn't I just pick some small area and do it thoroughly? Who, in short, did I think I was? I was so astonished by the way they were treating me that I could only gape. At the end, they told me to rethink my dissertation and come back in six months. Afterward Thomas Flanagan—who later wrote *The Year of the French*—took me aside. "Don't just sit there with that shit-eating grin on your face," he told me. "Get tough."

Six months later, not having changed a word, I went back. This time I dressed in black pants and a leather jacket, instead of my nice-girl dress, and combed my hair down over my eyes. When they challenged me, I spoke back. When I finished, they decided grudgingly to let me go ahead, and Tom Flanagan agreed to direct my thesis.

"We release you in the custody of your adviser," the head of my committee said, winking at Tom as though I were some sort of lunatic who had to be carefully watched. My second novel was getting some strangely similar reactions. Viking wrote me a long letter suggesting I cut out the selfish bitch and concentrate on the nice Jewish girl who has the baby. Evil didn't exist anymore as a concept, the editor explained. Though I said no to the rewrite, I was encouraged. Unlike the first novel, this one aroused considerable interest from major publishers. Christopher Lehmann-Haupt, then senior editor at Dial, wrote Toni that it was with real regret that he turned the book down. It was honest, well-written, and had great humanity, but he was afraid it was too quiet and uncommercial to sell.

While I was passing my doctoral exam and amassing rejections, Lisa had grown into a ravishing toddler with red curls. Though Richard didn't say much, I could see him looking proudly at her out of the corner of his eyes. He went with us to the zoo and held her up while she fed the animals. We went boating on Lake Merritt in Oakland and gave bread to the ducks. He read her *The Wind in the Willows* at night, surprising me by his brilliant acting of Toad. We bought a dog, a curly-haired neurotic Bedlington named Puck, who looked like a demented sheep. More important, we bought a house together. It was surrounded by pines, with high decks facing the bay.

I planted dwarf fruit trees on the decks, apple and peach and orange. I had a climbing structure made out of driftwood for Lisa to play on in the backyard. We watered the flowers in our new garden together and planted vegetables. Richard even planted radishes. We were a family.

When I told Richard I'd like to have another child, he said if that was what I wanted, fine. He told me the Talmud said a man should keep having children until he'd had four sons.

I was three months pregnant when Richard went night-wandering for the second time. It was the fall of 1965. We were in New York with Lisa, staying with my mother. When I woke up in the morning on the second day of our trip, Richard wasn't there. Mother was frantic. She called the police and reported a missing person. The policeman must have implied that Richard was probably just having himself a good time because I heard Mother say in her coldest Queen Victoria voice, "But he's a respectable man, a professor. He wouldn't have just gone off like that."

The officer laughed. "Have it your way, lady," he said, "but a person isn't missing until they've been gone twenty-four hours."

Richard came back to the apartment around nine in the morning, smoking a cigar and with a lazy, satisfied look on his face. When I asked him where he had been, he told me he'd stopped in at a bathhouse and fallen asleep. That was all. Nothing to make such a fuss about.

The next time he did this, I was less alarmed. I'd come across an essay by a famous analyst about how Jonathan Swift and Lewis Carroll, both supremely intellectual men, walked all night to calm their anxieties. Maybe it was the same with Richard. I came to accept his occasional nighttime excursions as a harmless eccentricity, a sign of his increasing professional restlessness.

For a while now, he'd been distressed by the events taking place on the campus. He hated the Free Speech movement and was increasingly isolated from most of his colleagues by his pro-war position on Vietnam: he insisted we had to keep fighting, that our withdrawal would lead to wholesale slaughter of the South Vietnamese. I refused to think deeply about it. I had literally stopped reading the newspapers after my father died. It was ironic. As a curious, engaged fourteen-year-old I had written reports on socialism and genocide and blamed my mother for her unworldliness. Now she was actively involved in civil rights, my brother was registering voters in Mississippi, and I simply wasn't interested in anything but my writing, my analysis, and my family. Of course, staying politically naïve kept me from fighting with Richard. But also, though he was saying things that sounded cruel, I really didn't believe he meant them. I took it as another sign of his intellectual ferment, his mind spinning off from his feelings.

Lisa's birth had taken fifteen hours; Michael was born fifteen minutes after I got to the hospital. He literally shot out into the doctor's hands. The doctor said he had never seen such an active baby. When I brought him home, Lisa hovered over him with interest, holding up his rattle or his teddy bear. The only thing that annoyed her was that I hadn't let her name him. I think she wanted to call him Jonathan.

"You should let her show her hostility," Maenchen said. "She's being too good."

"Maybe she likes him," I said. The last thing I wanted to do was pry out Lisa's hidden negative thoughts. She brought diapers for me, rocked Michael in his cradle. Told him stories she had heard at her Montessori preschool. Why would I want to spoil that?

When Michael was eight days old, we had him circumcised. I insisted it be done in a hospital, though I discovered later that the Jewish ritual circumcisers are more adept. I was horrified by the board on which Michael was tied like a trussed chicken and by the strength of his screams, but Richard was ecstatic at the birth of a Jew. "Now he's really a human being," he said.

In 1966, the year of the great flood of the Arno, we went back to Florence so Richard could finish his research. My dissertation was coming along smoothly—it almost wrote itself once my committee got out of my way—and I thought I could easily finish it while we were abroad. We rented the same villa on Viale Michelangelo that we had when Lisa was born. She went to a local nursery school up in the hills above Florence that had lots of green space for play and other American children who spoke English. The moment Lisa heard the taxi driver honk outside, she'd run for the door, yellow smock neatly buttoned, straw lunch box flying. Michael still slept a lot, and during his morning nap I'd write. Somewhere along the way, my second reader, Alexander Zwerdling, had pointed out that I was really writing a psychoanalytic study of Yeats, concentrating on his Oedipal problems. I didn't think I was doing anything so ambitious, but I didn't care how my thesis was defined at this point; I just wanted to be done with it. When Lisa came home, I would lay my work aside and we'd have lunch and go to the park with Michael in his stroller. Richard spent his days at the library.

One morning, I heard Pat, the wife of one of Richard's colleagues, calling beneath our window. She was pregnant with her fifth or sixth child.

"There's a flood," she screamed up to me. "The Arno's overflowed its banks." She was taking her children to the convent across the street.

"Oh, you know how women are," Richard said when I woke him. "They get hysterical if there's a drop of water on the floor."

With the best intentions and a wish to escape the worst of our pasts, we had somehow re-created them by now. Richard had taken on his father's sarcasms and I was often in a frenzy of anxiety over things ranging from the children's health to beetles crawling over my bare feet when we visited Ostia Antica. But I wasn't hysterical and neither was Pat, who for years had cared for a distracted husband and large family. Calling women hysterical was Richard's way of denying how dependent he really was on my steadiness. I was the one who dealt with everyday crises, from a child's toothache to a flood, so he could spend his time thinking serenely about his work.

I dressed Lisa; we put on our boots and went out in the pouring rain to see if there was in fact a flood. Lisa skipped alongside me, happy at the unexpected diversion. When we got to Via Orsini, where we usually went to buy chicken, there was no street, only a huge sheet of yellow water. A line of men in black slickers was stopping traffic coming down the hill. At the edge, where the water met the sharp uphill slope of the Viale, it was deceptively calm, lapping with gentle waves at our feet. Farther on, the yellow water still seemed placid enough until Lisa, screaming with excitement, spotted the top of an abandoned car protruding from the surface. I felt obscurely vindicated. Pat was right. The flood was all too real.

When Richard heard our news, he sent me up to the top of the Viale in our Fiat 600 to check out the extent of the flooding while he dressed and had breakfast. Florence is in a valley, a sort of bowl between hills. It was almost completely covered with yellow flood-water. Richard cursed when I told him the water was up over the steps of the library. I went back up the hill to buy supplies: bottled water—the radio said the tap water was unsafe—tinned meat, bread.

For the next week, we were trapped in our house, able only to drive to the top of the Viale. It was bitter cold. I tried to keep our furnace going, stoking it with coal the way I'd seen our maid, Elide, do, but one night it went out. The villa's walls exuded damp. I wrapped Lisa and Michael in all their clothes, and we had picnics on the kitchen table, where pots of boiling water took the chill off the room. Later, I used the water to bathe them, uncovering only a part at a time. I washed Michael's diapers in the stone sink, but because of the rain and the damp inside, they took forever to dry. It was hard, but I was pleased. I was stronger than I thought. Single-handed, I was keeping my family going.

At night, when I fell into bed too tired to sleep, I thought of writing a novel about a woman whose monotonous routine was broken into by a flood. Afterward there would be a new life. I had no trouble imagining the routine: nursing, diapering, shopping, feeding—with a few hours snatched for work. Equally easy to imagine was the husband and father: a man who was away at the library all day, coming back cranky or sarcastic. What I had trouble imagining was the new life. Right now, the only thing I could think of that would bring me and Richard close again was if I became an Orthodox Jewess, shaved my head, got a wig and joined him in prayer. He talked increasingly about moving us all to Israel, where we were going for a few weeks at the end of the sabbatical. I feared that he was starting to see making aliyah as a solution to his frustrations at the university.

So my sketch for the novel had us all ending up happy and holy in Jerusalem, but when I tried to flesh it out, the writing was stiff, and, though I couldn't see it, piously false. I woke up in the mornings, and looked at Richard sleeping next to me and tried to tell myself that my loneliness wasn't his problem. He provided for us, kept us sheltered and fed. We cared about different things, that was all. He was an old-style husband.

When the water finally went down, Richard worked knee-deep in mud, with the hundreds of volunteers who arrived from all over the world, to save the library's books and rare manuscripts. One day he came home and collapsed. He could barely move his legs. His joints were painfully inflamed. We had to get away from the damp. I piled the family into our Fiat and made for Rome, to the Pensione Villa Borghese, where we'd stayed before. The rooms were fairly spacious with high ceilings, and the waiters, Giuseppe and Giovanni, loved children. But our previous visits had been short. It was an entirely different matter for four of us to spend the winter months crammed into two rooms with a bath down the hall. There wasn't even a table, and there was no place at all to play.

Richard stayed flat on his back in bed, terrified that he had polio but unwilling to get medical attention. Doctors are almost as bad as lawyers, he'd say. Charlatans. Out for your money. He was a

grouchy, fretful patient; when I would ask him if he wanted anything or try to make him more comfortable, he'd snap, "Leave me
alone."

I tried to be understanding, but when he asked me to increase my
financial contribution to the household to help cover the extra hotel
expenses, I felt a surge of rage. I had often felt as though I was dependent, contributing nothing to the household. But in fact, besides
taking complete care of the children, I had been contributing $600 a
month from my trust fund income since we married. I covered all
the children's expenses, in addition to paying for my own clothes
and doctor's visits, as well as our joint vacations. Now there he was,
lying on his bed all day, complaining and wanting more money. A
little crack opened in my system of denial. But I still wasn't ready to
see my situation clearly. It was all I could do to see if it was nice
enough to take the kids to the park, or if the ice cream man was at
his corner.

I found a nursery school for Lisa, but on her first day the teacher
told her she'd cut off her thumb if she caught her sucking it again,
so I kept her home. I concentrated all my efforts on making her feel
this was fun. I bought her a beautiful red wool coat with a velvet
cap. Romans were very conscious of appearances and I didn't want
her snubbed for looking too much like a Berkeley child. Every day
when it wasn't raining we went to the park with Michael—also
dressed impeccably in hand-knit clothes—in his stroller.

If Lisa wasn't fully happy, at least she was getting by. She took
endless pony rides down the wide park avenues or rode a rented
bike with training wheels, and afterward we ate hot roasted chest-
nuts wrapped in paper cones. I sat in the sun with the other mothers
and nannies on the steps of the Villa Borghese and wondered
whether Richard was going to be a permanent cripple.

Once or twice I got the maid on our floor to watch the children
while I went out for an hour. She told Lisa she should pray to Baby
Jesus and gave her a little card with his picture. Richard threw a fit
when he saw it. "Never leave her in that woman's hands again," he
said. "Never." He'd made a mistake bringing us to this Catholic
country, he told me. Next time it would be Jerusalem. The proper
place for a Jewish child.

Richard didn't get better and finally I braved his curses and brought in a doctor to see him. The doctor gave him cortisone shots, and the inflammation went down almost immediately. We went back to Florence in March, Lisa returned to the nursery school she loved, and I finished my dissertation, typing much of it with Michael on my lap, then sent it off to the readers. In late May or June, we set off for Jerusalem for our two-week visit. We stayed in a hotel with a pool on the outskirts of the city right above an Arab village. Every day Richard would read the Hebrew paper and then stand looking down at the village. He thought he saw, he finally told me, the glint of guns. Somehow the threat of war that hung in the blue cloudless air seemed a fitting conclusion to our year of disaster. Something was building up that couldn't be stopped—in our marriage as well as in the world. First flood, then fire. On the advice of friends who told us the airport might be closed soon, we left abruptly, the day before the Six-Day War.

"You did really well," Maenchen told me when I saw her again. "You cared for your whole family without complaining. You didn't even get sick." She beamed at me as if this were her personal triumph. And in a way, it was. She had convinced me that I ought to sublimate my own needs to those of my family. And I had. I'd been strong, performed perfectly. And what's more, I was proud of it, too. After all, she was only reacting to what I was telling her. I must have related my story with an air of pleasure at my competence.

"I think you are ready to leave analysis," Maenchen concluded.

My being unhappy much of the time didn't seem to be an issue. In Rome, I had dragged the children with me to the hairdressers more times than I'd like to remember while I got elaborate hairdos, just for the relief of having someone's hands touching me in a caring way. But, even if I'd stressed that to Maenchen—which I didn't—I don't think it would have mattered. What was important was that I'd made the whole thing work. My unhappiness was irrelevant. According to Maenchen, I was cured. I had turned myself into the good woman so many classical analysts longed to create.

Chapter

11

*The great question that has never been answered
and which I have not yet been able to answer
despite my thirty years of research into the
feminine soul is "What does a woman want?"*
—SIGMUND FREUD

*T*wo years later, Lisa was in second grade at the local public
school, Michael was an energetic toddler, and I was longing to get
pregnant again. I craved the closeness, the urgently sucking mouth,
the eyes fixed on mine, the animal satisfaction of it. I wanted a new
baby with the same urgency that a freezing person would want to be
near a hot stove.

I was revising my dissertation as a book by then. I'd also gotten
part-time work teaching Yeats at UC Extension. The fact that it was
a tenuous job that could be terminated at any time suited me. I was
desperately afraid that if I threw myself into my career, I'd neglect
my children the way my mother had. In that respect getting pregnant again served as a perfect cover.

"Three children is a nice number," I explained to Maenchen
when I came back for what I tried to think of as a checkup, the way
you have regular visits after a bout with cancer.

"So is six," Maenchen snapped, not at all glad to see me back.

I couldn't understand why she was cross. Hadn't she always encouraged me to mother and nurture, to put my family ahead of my
career? Being pregnant, being a mother of young children, was one
thing I seemed to do well. Richard agreed that I was a good mother,
called me "Mommy" when he was in a good mood. Now, of
course, it is evident that Maenchen thought having another child
was a mistake given my difficulties in keeping Richard happy, but

she was determined not to point it out to me if I didn't see it. So she just gritted her teeth and talked to me about the female libido.

With my belly proclaiming my innocence of ambition, I worked hard at getting people like Frederick Crews, at that time a Freudian critic and one of the method's most famous practitioners, and Rudolph Binion, psychobiographer of Lou Andreas-Salomé, to read my manuscript, critique it, and in Fred's case recommend it to various presses. But it was done undercover, as it were. If you'd asked me what I was doing, I would have said, being pregnant. More to the point, I didn't need to see myself as an ambitious, bad, man-envying woman hankering to see her work in print. I was a nice, good, sweet, and—see, see, my belly—very pregnant woman.

For the first few months, I was blissfully happy. I sat on our deck overlooking the Golden Gate and drank in the colors of the trees. I even had some nice phone conversations with Mother about my plan to redecorate our guest room in sea-green like a grotto. Then I began to get fits of rage. I would lie awake at night hating my friend Barbara for forging ahead in her career, hating Richard for only thinking about himself, for sleeping on the couch after dinner when I wanted to talk and then going out for the rest of the night. I called Maenchen and asked if I could come back again for a refresher course. I knew I was supposed to be cured, but I felt I was backsliding. I was afraid I needed some regular sessions. My facade of cheerful performance was getting harder to keep up.

"I'm feeling angry a lot," I confessed apologetically as I eased back on her green couch. "Richard goes out several nights a week and doesn't come back until morning. Sometimes I imagine his car crashing on the bridge." I didn't tell her that the images of twisted and burning metal gave me a grim satisfaction, but maybe she guessed.

"What do you think he is doing?" she asked me.

"He says he's walking . . . or having a drink."

"Does that make you anxious?"

"Oh no," I said, sure that suspecting him would simply be a sign of bad character. "He's never been able to sleep." Besides I was reasonably sure he wasn't seeing a woman. He dressed badly when he went out and often wore trousers with stains on them. I couldn't imagine him meeting a woman looking like that.

"We'll just have to work your anger through again," she said, irritated at my refusal to be cured.

"When you're feeling affectionate to your husband," she would remind me, "you can tolerate his absences very well." She said the same thing about what she referred to as his "scoldings."

"You're right," I'd say, feeling abashed.

Or she'd take things back to my hostility to men, my envy of Richard's freedom. "You're angry that he gets to do what he wants, and you have to stay home and take care of the children," she would say, "but that is your job."

Actually Richard's bad behavior had been steadily escalating while Maenchen's responses stayed the same. Whenever Richard came home from being out all night he would berate me nonstop for leaving the burner on while I talked on the phone, or not screwing on the jar tops. The thrust of Maenchen's comments was always to increase my tolerance, never to tell me I had a right to be angry.

What Maenchen and I should have been talking about was not how I could tolerate his yelling better, but why I tolerated it at all. Now looking back, it's clear that his yelling struck me as a form of attention. When he treated me kindly, it made me nervous. "I'm more comfortable when he is severe," I wrote in my diary. "When he's too nice, I feel strange." My need for punishment and his to punish fed into each other. My trying harder just made him yell more. Tolerance wasn't a sign of health, it was a form of collusion.

"What do you mean you drove the car over some tracks?" I should have asked him, after he ripped the bottom out of our car. "Were you drunk, on drugs? And why were you in a deserted train station in the first place? What in God's name are you doing? I have to know, tell me."

I really didn't have the slightest idea who I'd married. Like my mother, Richard kept large parts of himself hidden. We each had roles to perform. I was acting my "good woman" part on a bare stage in my living room, while another script was being played out in the streets of San Francisco. While Richard lived his Circean nighttime life, things were not going to get better, no matter how much I analyzed my penis envy. What I should have been analyzing was what the payoff was in being so masochistic. Why did I have the crazy idea that his tormenting me was a sign of affection? That his only telling me he loved me when he was drunk showed how deep his love was? Why didn't I think I deserved someone who was nice to me?

After my divorce, when I complained to Eissler that Maenchen hadn't helped me, Eissler wrote: "You have to understand that analysts have a difficult problem when young children are involved. They can't take the responsibility of breaking a marriage. They try to protect it for the sake of the children." Oh.

But I can't blame it all on Maenchen. Being passive and vague about what was happening to my marriage obviously suited me in some way. Otherwise, why was I so passive for so many years? "Passivity" has become a dirty word, especially for women. No one can sympathize with a woman who won't take control of her life, who continually takes abuse—especially an educated woman, a woman with private means. I can hardly sympathize with her myself. But I'm stuck with her, if you see what I mean. She was me. And much as people try to deny that women like this still exist, they do.

In fact, being tolerant made me feel like a saint. And I liked it. Sainthood is addictive. Every time I gave up an impulse to strangle Richard, a streak of well-being coursed through my veins. "You are good," it sang.

The downside was that the buckets of anxiety I was carrying around got heavier and heavier. Since I couldn't afford to act anxious about Richard or be effectively angry at him, I worried continually about the children. Would Lisa make friends in school? Should I let her skip a grade? Was Michael too small, too thin? Did his having stomachaches all the time mean he was unhappy? I'm sure it drove Maenchen crazy to listen to me obsessing about them. She would beg me from time to time to use analysis more effectively. Though I dutifully brought in my dreams, she couldn't understand them. She wanted me to talk about how I felt about her.

"You don't seem to like me much," I said tentatively, when she pressed me. "I can hear it in your voice."

"My voice is just the same as ever," Maenchen said; she was cutting paper behind me and I could hear the snip of the scissors. "I wonder why you see me only one way, as a cruel, judgmental person."

I had the disloyal thought that she was a cruel, judgmental person.

"You see me as your superego," she said fretfully, "and you want to escape me. To act out your impulses."

I had an image of myself buying shoes for Michael, getting Lisa's glasses, soothing Richard when he came home in a temper, pulling things together, mediating—all the traditional female tasks. My continuing to be "cured" clearly meant continuing to do my female job without showing any signs that I was coming apart at the seams. What it amounted to was some Victorian ideal of duty. No wonder I thought of her as my conscience.

Though Maenchen insisted she didn't dislike me, I never felt she was entirely on my side. Particulary when it came to my work.

"Why this rush to write another book?" she asked me, when I told her that I was thinking of working on Blake next. "Always something more. You are afraid just to live." It's hard to convey the weary, almost funereal, tone in which she made her observations. Richard reinforced Maenchen's point with his macabre humor.

"What would a woman want with a book?" he would ask, rolling his eyes, whenever I made the mistake of talking about my ideas. (He had gotten the phrase from a science fiction story about a colony of grotesque breeding females.)

It had become clear to me, however, that writing focused me in a way that nothing else did. I had a different personality when I wrote, was sure of myself and my opinions. I never held back for fear of what some scholar or other would think. I didn't care. It was the one place where I could really be myself.

Maenchen kept hammering at my need for self-control. This was ironic because I was exerting the utmost control to stay on her couch and in my marriage—my "acting out," as she called it, was only the mildest symbolic protest. Several times I found myself reading the letters in people's trash and trying to imagine their stories. Someone else might have laughed and said, "I guess you think that's what analysts do, root around in other people's garbage. That's pretty funny. Maybe there is something you really want to do that you're not doing, like divorcing your husband or writing romances." But Maenchen just told me to stop doing it.

It occurs to me now that maybe she was right to worry so much about my small lapses of control. They meant, for one thing, that I was no longer trying desperately to win her approval by presenting myself as competent and in control the way I had after the flood. Now, I was suggesting instead that my situation was untenable. Something was definitely changing. Maenchen felt it and tried hard to keep the lid on.

"Freud says women have deficient superegos, you know," she told me. "But why do you see me as yours? Who was this, who was this in your past?"

"I dunno," I said dully, "maybe my mother?" Well, in my early twenties, I'd been afraid of my impulses. Afraid I was getting too cruel, too spoiled, too promiscuous. I'd wanted someone to take me in hand, hadn't I? Now I had two people trying to do it. Richard and Maenchen.

Under her scrutiny, my self-control seemed to get worse by leaps and bounds. One day I reported that I had been sorely tempted to steal a zucchini squash from the university-sponsored children's garden in Strawberry Creek. It was big and green and would have been delicious sliced thin and fried. In Maenchen's opinion it was also the big prick my mother failed to give me at birth. And which I had to stop wanting.

"If you had done that, Mrs. Vebster," she hissed, "I would really have given up hope for you."

The more frustrated and impotent I felt, the more punitive she got.

"Why haven't you gotten any better in all these years when you have had such excellent therapists as me and Dr. Eissler?" she asked. "I don't understand it."

"Maybe you're not as good as you think you are," I said, goaded beyond endurance. She went dead on me. No sound, not even a grunt. And it took away my fire. I simply couldn't tell her I wasn't coming back. Not yet. First I had to make her talk to me. "Sorry," I mumbled. "It's just that it's upsetting me, too."

"Some people never get better, no matter how talented their analysts are," she said, "like Marilyn Monroe. Eight analysts tried to help her, but she was empty inside. Still, I can't decide whether you are really hopeless or whether you're just pretending. Imitating your crazy mother."

"If I'm only imitating, then I suppose I could change," I said, helpfully, "imitate someone else." I knew she'd love it if I said, "like you," if I broke down and admitted that she was my ideal. But desperate as I was for a soft word from her, I couldn't do it.

According to theory, Maenchen and I were working through childhood traumas via transference: her "coldness" was the way I experienced my mother; eventually, I'd see it, and be released from my groveling slavery. But we obviously weren't working through anything.

Meanwhile, my belly grew larger, and in June 1969 I gave birth to a second daughter, Rebecca Gabrielle. I had gotten so good at natural childbirth that I didn't even have to have an episiotomy: she just slid out. They put her to my breast and she immediately started sucking with the energy that has characterized her ever since. Afterwards with her smelling warm and milky nestled beside me in her yellow receiving blanket, I ate a steak dinner. I felt great. Even Maenchen was impressed with how unneurotic I was about giving birth, though it didn't make her reconsider her grim thoughts about my deficiencies.

I used to think my experience with Maenchen was unique, but in recent years have learned differently. At least two writers I admire said they'd had similar experiences with Maenchen. One of these writers, Jack Last, said that Maenchen told him he'd never be able to love anyone and continually put him down. A friend of his, Laura Blum, had a similar experience with a male analyst named Windholz. Laura thought certain older analysts used purposely harsh methods. An analyst acquaintance confirmed this.

"They thought some people just wouldn't change unless you confronted them," she said. She told me how Windholz reported rebuking a male patient for being a perpetual adolescent.

"But I'm in a depression," the man said, "how can you say something like this to me?"

"Because I don't have time to wait for you to change," Windholz answered.

"That's just the way these old analysts were," my acquaintance said wryly. "It was a little like being analyzed by your grandfather. We all discounted it. But if you started with Maenchen at twenty-five, if no one told you about it and you had nothing to compare it with, it could have been traumatic.

"None of this would be coming out if some of the older analysts like Anya hadn't died. But some are still alive. Anna Freud was harsh too," she said after thinking a moment, "and Anya Maenchen was analyzed by her. So it's natural she'd be that way too. But you're lucky you had her. It was like having a direct line from Anna Freud. You must have learned so much."

I mentioned this conversation to another friend, a senior analyst at the Psychoanalytic Institute. "Anya was destructive," he said sadly. "She was an insecure person." Too bad for me.

After Becca was born, my mother came to visit, as she had after each child's birth. She was in a final period of creative energy before her health began to fail. She had been doing a series of pregnancy paintings to celebrate my and my sister-in-law's pregnancies, along with huge mythic canvases in which she finally seemed to be coming to terms with my father's death. We had some good talks about Blake's drawings, which I was beginning to try to interpret, but by now she and Richard were getting along badly. Though she'd set herself to be calm and friendly—under Kris's direction—Richard responded with frigid politeness. Mother's anxiety grew accordingly and we were all in a state of jangled nerves by the end of the visit.

Some weeks later, I got a letter from Bernard Kendler at Cornell telling me that they would consider publishing my book on Yeats with some extensive rewriting. If I were going to rework my book with a broader, more sophisticated framework, I felt I needed a more thorough grounding in recent theory, and I decided to apply to the San Francisco Psychoanalytic Institute for training.

It would be exciting to see creative people as patients; I thought listening to them would allow me to see for myself just how true psychoanalytic theory—particularly about women—was. By now I had my doubts. I was also sick to death of being beaten up on by Maenchen and felt there might be a chance of escape if I could change my status from patient to apprentice. Certainly, I wanted to see what it was like being on the other side. Identification with the aggressor, the shrinks would say.

As part of the application, we had to write biographical statements. This was always hard for me. I couldn't find the proper voice and sounded naïve, like a nice, sweet little girl, rather than anyone with a mind. Ten years ago, my eldest daughter read my graduate school application for the Woodrow Wilson fellowship—she had found it in a trunk—and burst out laughing. "'I want to get to know mankind,'" she read between gasps of laughter. "Was that biblically or otherwise? Oh, Mom . . . you didn't have a clue."

Two friends of mine, Joe and Estelle Weiss, talked over my application with me. Joe was a classmate of Richard from Harvard, a brilliant, somewhat abstract man. His wife, Estelle, had been analyzed by Maenchen (whom Estelle now admits she didn't like) and was a training analyst at the institute. Estelle and Joe had already encouraged me to sample the institute's courses on applied psychoanalysis—the only ones open to qualified outsiders—and I'd taken several of them. There were some particularly interesting case presentations relating patients' traumas to elements in their art. I told Joe I was worried that having a suicidal mother who'd been in analysis for twenty years would be a drawback. Joe reassured me—everybody has something they're ashamed of. The main thing is to be absolutely honest.

Looking back, I was clearly a bundle of insecurities. I not only believed in the gulf between "them" and me—"they" being sane and strong and I being a weak defective from bad stock—but, worse, I believed in "their" supernatural powers. I actually believed that my examiners would know what I didn't tell them. Around this time I made friends with Jeffrey Masson. He had read some of my preliminary work on Blake and invited me to his house to give a presentation. He took me out to lunch and told me not to worry about my interview. In his opinion, most of the analysts couldn't see an inch in front of their noses.

My interviews were probably fairly standard. Robert Wallerstein (who later became a friend) asked me about my grasp of theory and whether I thought I could manage the intellectual side of the program. Herbert Lehman, director of the education committee, talked to me in a sensitive way about how I thought training might enrich my own work.

But there were some comic moments. One interviewer asked me if I thought I was going to change the field with my contributions.

"No," I said. "I doubt it." (Did I really look like a megalomaniac?)

"Oh," he said, "then you're just going on with the same old thing?" He was sitting in a straight-backed chair and I was seated in front of him in a chair that tilted me awkwardly backward. I should have asked him what he was driving at but, tilted back as though I were in a dentist's chair, all I could manage was, "Well, yes, more or less the same thing." (A poor thing, my lord, but mine own.)

Another interviewer asked me if I had any hidden physical defect. "Why?" I asked him.

"Well, because you're friends with Estelle Weiss and she has an eye that wanders. I thought maybe you had something similar."

"Not that I can think of," I said, unable to follow the logic, "unless small breasts qualify as a defect." I meant it as a sort of joke. He didn't laugh.

Joe had warned me that Emmy Sylvester could be difficult. She was an analyst of Maenchen's vintage with the same heavy accent and abrasive manner, gimlet eyed. She'd worked with Bruno Bettelheim at his famous school for autistic children.

She opened with the equivalent of a mental rabbit punch. "And why, Mrs. Vebster, are you applying to the institute now when you have a suckling infant at home?"

A friend, Nancy Chodorow, told me that when she applied a few years after me, she refused to answer questions they wouldn't ask a male candidate. But though feminist consciousness was being raised in the 1960s, I had been too busy with children and work to notice.

Sylvester narrowed her eyes incredulously when I explained how I thought working with patients would deepen my interpretations of texts, make them less abstract.

"Are you interested in child analysis?"

"I think it is a fascinating field," I stammered. "I love Bettelheim's work." I sputtered to a halt hearing myself. Under her fierce stare, I couldn't think of anything intelligent to say.

"I think you really want to become a child analyst," she said finally. "It seems to me you are being opportunistic here, wanting to use the institute for your own purposes."

The word "opportunistic" hurt. I repeated it to myself. Opportunistic. Sure, I wanted to take advantage, make the most of my abilities.

When I called to find out what had happened to my application, I was told in a kindly way that there had been considerable discussion, but that the committee had decided it would be best not to disrupt a going thing: I was writing successfully—I had told them I had other projects in mind—and I could always consult with them if I needed to. They weren't sure I realized how much time and energy training would take up. I had a young family. . . .

Despite the gentleness of their reply, I felt flattened. It was as if Maenchen and Sylvester had conspired to keep me prone on the couch, turning my love of being a mother into a handicap.

Richard was gleeful. He hated the idea of my becoming a lay analyst. While I was applying to the institute, he decided that six months in Israel in the coming spring of 1970 would do us good. He was thinking of emigrating and this would give him a chance to see what Hebrew University was like. If I had had a job, or had been admitted to the institute, I might have felt justified in saying I didn't want to go. But not now.

By this time religion had become a major issue. Richard read Hebrew newspapers for hours everyday and studied Torah on Saturdays with his friend Bob. Our interests almost never converged, but once over dinner I mentioned that Swedenborg's mystical visions seemed pretty nutty.

"Swedenborg isn't crazy," Richard snapped back. "Your mother is crazy because she can't balance a checkbook. Swedenborg's visions enhanced his ego; they were good for him."

Our belief systems were clashing. Richard was always attacking psychoanalysis for being a cult, an inferior version of a real religion. I—though I was suffering from my analysis with Maenchen—always responded with a sort of knee-jerk defense. I'm sure he felt that if I hadn't had psychoanalysis he would have won me over to commitment as a Jew. Right after we married, he had entreated me with great eloquence to return to "Abraham our father and Sarah our mother." It was ironic, really, because psychoanalysis was keeping me in line almost as well as being an Orthodox Jewish woman would have.

The two belief systems actually share more than is observable at first glance. They are both intensely male-oriented, for one thing. They both agree that women are defective and not full partners in the social order—at best they are helpmates and breeders. Freud thought that too much "intellectual training" could lead women to forget their feminine function—sexuality and intellect were basically opposed. Rational progressive qualities are all associated with the male. The aim of cure for a man was to develop and free his capacities, for a woman simply to resign her to her sexuality. Though, paradoxically, women were prominent in the early days of the psycho-analytic movement, they were lieutenants rather than leaders. When someone like Karen Horney tried to point out irrationalities in Freud's theories of early development—how they sounded like the crowing of a four-year-old boy over his penis—she was harassed.

Richard should have been grateful for Maenchen's surveillance since he was worried I'd bolt the marriage. He said he'd be relieved when I turned fifty because then I'd be too old to run away. But what he called the Freudian Bible set his teeth on edge. On bad days he referred to my work—psychoanalyzing texts—as shit and on good ones he simply ignored it. He was outraged at the amount of money my mother wasted on analysis.

"Your mother is throwing your money down the drain," he'd say, his face contorted with anger.

I was just as unhappy about his overriding concern with being Jewish. I couldn't understand why observance was so important when as far as I could see he didn't even believe in God. Not in some white-bearded old man in the sky, he told me, but there were forces in the Universe that none of us understood. Anyway, the beauty of Judaism was that you didn't have to believe, you just had to do the actions, light the candles, say the prayers.

Though I complained, I often enjoyed doing these things. But I couldn't forget that in back of the prayers was the premise that women were second-rate, if not outright dangerous. They were seg-regated in the Hasidic synagogue we attended, sitting behind a pan-el, unable even to see the rabbi. The direct link to God is through the male and every morning he puts on tefillin—a prayer strap—and thanks God that he was not born a woman. To make sure I got the message, Richard was fond of quoting Milton's famous line about Adam and Eve—"He for God only, she for God in him"—and re-minded me that there was room for only one ego in our household: his.

Richard had a complicated attitude toward Judaism. He suffered from it—often he was intensely irritated by his fellow Jews—but he couldn't detach himself. He thought people who assimilated—and here he would name his most detested colleagues—had impover-ished themselves. He made every effort to ensure that the children would feel the same way. It was really the only area of their lives in which he took a deep interest. He had started Lisa on informal Hebrew lessons. Going to Israel would consolidate what she had learned.

My first reaction to the idea of spending six months in Israel was panic. It would mean putting any rewrite of my Yeats book on hold. I wouldn't have the libraries I needed for my research. And as always when we traveled, I would be devoting my energy to making the children feel comfortable. I had a gruesome dream of Richard's mother hacking his father to bits with an ax. In penance, I went out and bought myself three years' worth of the books they use in Israel to teach new immigrants Hebrew. "*Motig*—sweetness," I wrote in my diary. "*Hamuda*—nice." Just what I wasn't.

I liked Israel better than I thought I would. During our first days at Eilat, in January 1970, at the Red Sea, touring the territories won in the Six Day War—miles of sand under a burning sun—I noticed how the young soldiers, men and women, sauntered about equally burnished and confident. This was secular Israel, as far from the ultra-Orthodox synagogue in Berkeley as it was from the Hasidic quarter in Jerusalem. I could identify with these young men and women much more easily than I could with the praying, swaying Jews in the synagogues. These were regular people and, more important, they didn't look like victims. No one was going to shove these people into ovens without a struggle. I liked that. Even in that first encounter, I felt the sense of hope in a young country. It was brash, unwelcoming even—a sea filled with coral that slashed your feet—but it was determined to grow.

Our apartment was in Beit Hakarem, a suburb of Jerusalem. It was a nice, light apartment with a small terrace. There were parks where the children could play, and a supermarket down the block. Richard planned to go to the university by bus. There was no need for a car, he told me. Everything I needed was in walking distance. I could put Becca in my baby carrier and do my shopping. He arranged for me to have Hebrew lessons from someone in the neighborhood; Michael's kindergarten was next door and Lisa's school a few blocks away.

People could be madly abrasive, pushy, annoying, aggressively militant, but there was also a freshness and spontaneity about them. There was a general air of danger. Children were warned not to pick up small objects in the street or on the playground because they might be grenades. But every time there was a holiday, the children would dress up and celebrate with banners and singing and dancing in the streets. I'd see the kids dancing and tears would come to my eyes. In Israel, at that time, loving your country seemed all right.

Every day Michael and Lisa went off to school and I sat home and nursed Becca—a robust baby with a strong sense of her rights.

At Lisa's school they made the children speak only in Hebrew to hasten the absorption of new immigrants. Since Lisa knew only a few words, she stopped talking and was put back a grade. It must have seemed like a punishment. Her sweet face wore a permanent, puzzled frown. When she came home from school, I read her *Ozma of Oz* to cheer her up.

Luckily, Michael loved his kindergarten teacher, a black-haired woman with an amazing figure who used to carry him around and sing to him.

"I learned to kiss on the lips," he told me happily one day. That was fine with me. It was long before teachers were accused of child molesting. When he wasn't practicing his kissing, he dressed up as a cowboy or a biblical character and whooped or danced.

Richard was pleased by the children's exposure to Hebrew but bitterly disappointed with the infighting between his colleagues at Hebrew University. He thought Jews ought to be better than everyone else, especially in moral matters. They should set an example for the goyim. It infuriated him that the intellectuals didn't understand Israel's responsibility to be a light to the Nations. Meanwhile, he wasn't in a mood to listen to any complaints from me: the slightest comment about Lisa's misery at school sent him into a rage. He treated anything that went wrong at home, even illness, as purposely designed to thwart him.

On Passover, Richard ended the service with the Song of Songs, which he always interpreted as showing God's love for Israel. His disappointment in the daily reality of Israel made this symbolic representation all the more important, and he read it with tears in his eyes while I sat glumly thinking about my Yeats book, which had been rejected by Wesleyan the day before: "Brilliant but unscholarly."

Lisa was old enough to sit quietly during the four-hour reading, but Michael crept away and started playing under the coffee table.

Richard blamed me for not keeping things together. "They're children," I said, "not robots."

Later, in our bedroom, he wondered aloud whether he should divorce me. "I don't know," I said gloomily. "It's obvious you're dissatisfied with me. I'm not a good Jewish wife. But at least I pay my share of our expenses." In another couple this would have escalated into a full-scale fight. And things would have come out into the open. But I didn't have the energy to fight. I just damped things down. I was becoming a marital zombie.

I felt that my miseries were only ordinary piffling middle-class ones. There were people all around me who had been through unimaginable hell and survived. My Hebrew teacher, Haddasah Rhem, for instance—a Dutch woman with a gentle, husky voice who came to Israel from the extermination camps—didn't seem damaged, she seemed tempered as fine steel. She and her husband lived in a little shack, but they spoke of Israel in hushed tones as "*Gan Eden*" and in a universal spirit worked to forge bonds with their Arab neighbors.

Another Israeli friend, Irene Eber, a woman who taught Chinese at Hebrew University, had survived during the war by hiding for two years in a chicken coop. Afterward she had to relearn how to speak. When the war was over, she adopted a Chinese child and fought the discrimination against her for adopting a non-Jewish child.

"Haven't they learned anything?" she asked me. "They know what it feels like. How can they persecute other people? How?"

"I guess some people learn from experience and some don't," I said. It was a cliché, but suddenly I understood something. Suffering wasn't an excuse for hurting other people. Or for letting yourself be hurt. I wanted to be someone who learned. Someone who changed and did things differently.

Chapter

12

*In motherhood, as it is structured, circumstances
for sustained creation are almost impossible . . .
Motherhood means being instantly interruptible,
responsive, responsible. . . . The very fact that
these are needs of love, not duty, that one feels
them as one's self, that there is no one else to be
responsible for these needs, gives them primacy.
It is distraction, not meditation, that becomes
habitual. . . .*

—TILLIE OLSEN

Once when my younger daughter, Rebecca, was in high school, I
showed her my files of reviews for my Yeats book.

"They think you're good," she said amazed. "Why didn't you tell
me?"

"You knew I was writing books."

"But you acted so ditzy. I never thought they'd be—you know—
good."

Shortly after I came back from Israel, I started noticing that I was
split into two people. Yeats's concept of the self and the anti-self got
me thinking about it. One of my selves would write extraordinary
things—possibly winning the Pulitzer Prize like my cousin George
Oppen—but always in secret. The other would go on—in a daze of
tiredness—helping the children with their homework.

I could switch from one self to another at the snap of a finger.
While I was deeply concentrating in my study, Lisa came in carrying
Becca in her arms. "See, Mama's here," Lisa said sweetly, taking on
a maternal voice. Instantly the competent woman vanished and a
sweet vague mothering self took her place.

Besides starting work on a new framework for my book, I found
time to make one of my chapters on Yeats's early style into an article. I sent it to Eissler, who after shooting off a cranky response

about doing wild analysis—making suppositions about a person I didn't have on the couch—later suggested I send the essay to a friend, Harry Slochower, at *American Imago*. When Slochower accepted the piece, Eissler graciously said that his own shortcomings had made him critical and that he trusted this was only the beginning for me.

For me, it was a momentous occasion. It was not only my first publication, but my former analyst was no longer telling me to go into my garden and sniff the roses. He was actually supporting my work.

Even stronger support came from a training analyst at the institute, Estelle Weiss—Joe's wife—who began coaching me on the finer points of psychoanalytic theory to help me with my work on Yeats. For the next year and a half, she winnowed out the theoretical wheat from the chaff and presented it to me. Besides being brilliant, she was funny and irreverent. While telling me about pre-Oedipal phenomena, she would suddenly break out into a little song, "Here we go searching for primal scenery/among California's mountain greenery." Most of what they learned at the institute was useless, Estelle told me. The main conceptual advance that she thought would be helpful to me in thinking about Yeats's symbols and their function in his psychic life was Winnicott's work with transitional objects: objects like the child's teddy bear that are experienced as an extension of the self.

She was wonderfully generous with her time and effort, and I grew to love her in the way that patients are supposed to love their analysts—the way transference is ideally supposed to work. Sometimes I felt as if Estelle were enabling me to start over again as a child, seeing things in a new way. I wrote poems in which I worried that she would go away and leave me abandoned in a world without color or meaning.

I couldn't really go through childhood again—it was too late for that—but I could still grow in understanding, and my work became part of a process of growth. I used it to understand things about myself at one remove. It functioned better for me than my official work with Maenchen; in fact my literary work was the only place in my life where psychoanalysis had a positive impact.

Yeats's main problem was a sort of dreamy passivity—so was mine. My curiosity about the way he worked his way out of it

The Last Good Freudian

gave me the energy to plow through reams of boring theoretical papers searching for clues. I began to see that his passivity was part of a defense system that didn't work very well. As he grew older, he found better means of protecting himself. He invented concepts and images like his Golden Bird that he used to make himself stronger, not just in his poetry but in his life. The revelation for me was that growth as an artist doesn't have to be at the expense of the lived life.

By spring 1971, I was ready to write a new conclusion to my Yeats book, which was now clearly about transformation and change. I turned my new final chapter into an article on "Sailing to Byzantium" and a friend, Murray Baumgarten, invited me to give it as a paper at the University of California at Santa Cruz. Norman O. Brown, then at the height of his fame as a guru, was in the audience. I had heard he could be a devastating critic, but he was courtly and complimentary. Hearing that I was revising my book for Cornell, he offered to write them a letter on my behalf. This was another milestone. I had bypassed the usual route of a job, publication, tenure, and was getting to speak from outside.

While I was waiting to hear from Cornell after doggedly submitting my revised manuscript for yet a third time, I looked for something to occupy me. My friend Joan Lester told me she needed a research assistant, someone who was willing to go up every day and take notes on the behavior of young adolescent female langurs. Joan, a professor of physical anthropology at Berkeley, had spent years in India studying these sleek, gray-brown monkeys with faces like mournful Madonnas. Something about it intrigued me. I sensed that I needed to get some distance on the habit of caretaking. Sure, I told Joan. I'd like to see how the langurs socialize their young. They are our closest cousins, after all.

All through September 1972, I learned how langurs communicate with each other. How they signal their desire to play, be groomed, or, most rarely, have sex. It was very civilized. Like Richard and me: they knew their places and kept to them. There was a dominant male, Big Horse, and a dominant female, Big Mama, and then a line of subordinates down to the weakest member. The langurs didn't fight much. They had an elaborate series of gestures—baring the teeth in a parodic smile was my favorite—to indicate that a fight might ensue if someone didn't back off.

147

Once a whole group of young males got into trouble with Big Horse for playing too close, and he gave them a serious threat. They backed off, their heads to the ground.

"It's like a tenure committee meeting," I whispered to Joan. She didn't find it funny. She just wanted me to stick to the facts.

Traditional langur lore had it that when a baby was born the young females would all cluster around and take turns babysitting. That's how they learned their role. But during my shifts, the langur adolescents—and some of their mothers—would show distinctly unfeminine behavior. First, Bouncer, instead of making love with her father, Big Horse—an event I had looked forward to with prurient curiosity—chased him around and around the cage. Young females are not supposed to chase grown males, but no one lifted a brow ridge. Big Horse seemed faintly surprised, but he ran. Bouncer was clearly a neurotic young monkey. When she wasn't chasing Big Horse, she was bouncing up and down or looking out at me from between the bars. "Hey pal," I whispered to her when Joan wasn't looking, "maybe you have the right idea."

The next to show deviant behavior was Smooth, a sleek adolescent, in collusion with a mother, Girl, who wasn't acting right either. She had given birth to a male—an adorable creature who clung to her breast and looked around with huge dark eyes. Langur females are programmed to respond to their infants' distress cries, which have roughly three levels of intensity. The last and loudest usually gets an immediate response. Everything started well. Smooth, taking her turn as babysitter, cradled the infant in her arm and looked at it tenderly. But after a few minutes she seemed to get bored. The adolescent males and one other female were playing tag in one corner of the cage, and she kept eyeing them as if she wanted to play, too. Tentatively she began rocking the baby harder, up and back, as she ran alongside the group that was playing. The infant started to squeak in distress. But when I looked over at its mother, Girl was eating bananas companionably in a group of females and didn't seem to notice. Smooth swung harder and started to throw the baby up in the air as if it were a ball. Loud shrieks. The mother didn't respond. As I watched, Smooth's movements got more and more violent until the baby accidentally hit its head against a climbing pole. A few days later, I heard that it had died.

We weren't supposed to interfere with the monkeys, and, even if I had wanted to, it went by too fast. But somehow, and this was the awful part, the experience was cathartic. Had the monkey done what so many overstressed caretakers, including me, are afraid they'll do? Bash a baby's brains out?

When Girl delivered a second infant, she wouldn't nurse it. She had to be tranquilized with a blow dart and put in a small cage, her infant clinging to her breast, where she couldn't escape her responsibilities.

"How do you explain it," I asked Joan, "women's liberation?" I was joking to cover the fact that I was totally confused by my reactions. Joan just walked away with a grim expression.

Drenched by guilt over my identification with Smooth and Girl, I went over to my friend Channa's house and watched her nurse her baby. It was a relief to feel the stir of hormones. I had loved nursing, I told Channa. I loved the way the baby's eyes locked on mine and stayed there. I loved everything about it.

No one talks about being a nursing addict. There is great sensual pleasure, for one thing, a groggy warmth. But more important for someone who feels inadequate, there is the joy of giving another creature total satisfaction. Nothing matches it except the best possible sex. When I saw Channa nursing, I had to fight the impulse to rush home and get pregnant again.

Becca, already a three-year-old delighting in clothes and what she called her "jools" (jewelry), had started Montessori preschool. So much free time meant I could concentrate more on myself. But it also made me panic because underneath an inchoate fear was building up that my work would endanger my children. After resubmitting my manuscript to Cornell, I had written a poem about my mother painting my portrait and skewering my smile, transferring it to her canvas, leaving me with a blank face. I thought at the time the poem was about my mother's coldness, her involvement in her art somehow negating me, but now I think it was also about my fear of actually succeeding and being recognized. More important, having to recognize—because it would then be public—that the self who wrote the book was the same one who mothered the children. It would, as it were, blow my cover.

In December 1972, Cornell rejected my book yet again. Apparently they had asked their reader if the book would be a classic and he said no, it would be superseded, though it was a pioneering work. I was furious. Since when was being a classic necessary for publication?

Jess Bell at Stanford agreed to look at the book, and asked Bernard Kendler at Cornell to give him the name of the writer of the positive report. Kendler said that was confidential information. My frustration galvanized me into doing something unusual. I asked Kendler to give my name to the reader and ask him to identify himself to me and help me out. The reader turned out to be Harold Bloom, one of the most influential critics in the country; he strongly recommended my book to Stanford.

When my book was accepted by Stanford, I had a surge of hope for myself. Richard didn't rejoice, but he didn't say anything nasty, either. For a while he simply ignored what had happened.

Feeling encouraged, I wrote to Phyllis Greenacre, one of the old-guard Freudian analysts especially interested in creativity, asking her if, as I had heard, she were still working on Blake. There would have been no point in two psychoanalytic studies. While I was waiting to hear if the field was clear, I wrote an article on a medieval poem that had always fascinated me, *Sir Gawain and the Green Knight*.

I was only minimally aware of feminism and its historical reinterpretations, but through the back door of psychoanalysis I was drawn to investigate the same problems. The poem had a clear oedipal theme, which had never been noticed. But beyond that, what interested me was its misogyny and the way religion reinforced the feudal system of male allegiances. In the odd way intellectuals have of doing things at a distance, I was thinking about my marriage and the ways it fit a cultural pattern.

Greenacre wrote me that she had given up her project and invited me to visit her. Meanwhile, Estelle agreed to help me again. She was very excited. Blake had been a love of hers for a long time. Though I wanted it very much, my limited success frightened me, and in a variety of ways I tacked back and forth. This would go on for the next couple of years. I would keep losing my Blake notes and, like Penelope, have to keep redoing everything from scratch.

My fear of harming the children came back. I started worrying about them obsessively, particularly about Lisa, who was teetering on the verge of adolescence and didn't seem happy.

I went back to see Maenchen, whom I hadn't seen for four years, since I had been pregnant with Becca. It is almost as if I had a quota of worry and guilt that had to be filled. If my work was going too well, it made me worry doubly about the children. Besides, my mother hadn't wanted me to separate and do things successfully on my own. Maybe, odd though it sounds, I rushed back to reassure Maenchen that I couldn't manage without her. Maenchen encouraged me to review my past once again. But without a grasp of the real issues, she went astray.

There were two central points to the psychic story that Dr. Maenchen had constructed for me. The first was of course oedipal. I had been a rival with my mother for my father's love and had consistently lost out because she was so much more beautiful and talented. The second was penis envy and competition with my brother. Because of my history of competition with Chris, Maenchen now saw me as pressuring Lisa to excel. For years Maenchen had told me that my guilt and bad feelings about myself came from penis envy, which, she said, also provided much of the energy behind my drive to work.

At this point, though, I didn't need to hear again about why my work had bad motives. If anything, I needed to be encouraged to think better, not worse, of myself. As for Lisa's unhappiness, how could I not have seen that it was a result of the tension in our household? How could she feel good about herself when she saw me being treated like a dishrag and responding with a mindless "Yes, dear." Richard reinforced the effect by calling her a slob, just like her mother. No wonder she didn't want to be around me or us, wanted to go to boarding school in the country and raise sheep.

"You can be creative in so many ways as a housewife," Maenchen intoned, "but you aren't satisfied with that. You want Lisa to be something more." And it's true, I did. Though I didn't see the extent to which Lisa suffered from our marital difficulties, some doubts started to creep in. Would it be better, I wondered, if I left him? Maenchen was neutral. "The woman holds the family together and creates the atmosphere," she told me. "That is the truly creative function of the female libido. If it becomes impossible, you separate and do it for the children."

Impossible? My reaction was to gulp for air and decide to keep going.

In the fall of 1973, we were in Italy again. I hadn't wanted to go in the first place. I wanted to be home and celebrate the publication of my book: *Yeats: A Psychoanalytic Study*. I also wanted to start work on Blake.

Also, though I'd sidestepped the issue of leaving Richard, I dreaded being isolated again in a foreign country. On the other hand, I couldn't seem to get rid of a flicker of hope that something would change and we'd find ourselves happy. Richard wasn't uniformly cranky. Before we left Berkeley, he'd even arranged for me to have a job interview with a colleague at Cal. I didn't get the job because I hadn't studied *Beowulf*, but I was touched.

One day soon after we arrived in Rome, when we'd just consumed huge platters of *pasta con funghi* washed down with red wine and I thought he looked mellower than usual, I asked him what I could do to help our marriage.

"You could be more like Pat Nixon," he said. "There's a woman who helps her husband's career."

I almost laughed. There was something comical about the way he made even his most outrageous statements, almost as if he were doing a parody of a macho role, but then I saw that he was grinding his teeth.

"You know I'm interested in your work," I offered. We were in Italy this time so Richard could dig up some new facts about Gabriele D'Annunzio, the Italian aviator, poet, and friend of Il Duce. D'Annunzio was also a compulsive Don Juan, an incredibly arrogant and self-centered man.

"You're interested as a competitor," Richard said. "You think you understand him better than I do. You don't care about me at all. You only care about your psychiatrist and the children."

Perhaps if he'd said it less angrily, I could have heard how left out he felt.

"I wouldn't have read D'Annunzio at all if you hadn't asked me to," I said defensively. "You wanted me to help you with the literary stuff." Naturally I had found all sorts of psychological themes. It was obvious that D'Annunzio was afraid of women. He made his heroes do ghastly things to them, like cutting off their hands or pushing them off cliffs, so they couldn't drain the heroes' vital powers through sex.

Richard hated my ideas at the time, but fifteen years after our divorce he would begin a psychobiography of D'Annunzio.

When a copy of my Yeats book reached me in Rome along with the first reviews, Richard turned it facedown and locked it in a glass cabinet in the living room of our apartment. He ignored the good reviews Jess Bell sent—including a lead article in *The New Republic*—and smirked when a reviewer in *The London Times* implied I was an "opinionated bitch."

I felt too guilty at my good fortune in being published by Stanford to do more than murmur. Jess Bell had rejected Richard's second book after he refused to cut it. I'd argued with Richard, pleaded, but no one was going to tell him anything about his prose. Now he felt betrayed.

When Richard's book was accepted by the University of California Press a month or so after mine came out, I ran to him with the heavy manila envelope containing the contract. I hoped that he'd be less angry with the world, that his litany of complaints about his colleagues and my defects would decrease. But now, after opening the envelope, he told me in a way that felt genuine how disappointed he was with his life. Starting with the Free Speech movement, everything had gone wrong for him at Berkeley: standards declined, his colleagues didn't respect him, used him "as a garbage pail for their problems." His best friend Joe died in a tragic accident.

In retrospect, it seems clear Richard was in a downward spiral. Israel hadn't worked for him—his dreams of a life there were shattered. And now he had to face competition from me. He ended by saying he could never forgive me for stabbing him in the back by submitting my book to Stanford. Since then, he had been flooded with rage ten times a day.

In the past when I'd seen him contorting his face, and asked him what was the matter, he'd always say, "Nothing." I'd twisted myself into knots trying to understand what went on in his mind. Now, listening to him tell me how hurt and disappointed he was, I felt a surge of love and pity. I offered again to help him with D'Annunzio.

For the next couple of months, I went off to the archives for a couple of hours every day to read the newspapers of D'Annunzio's Fiume period, when he was commandant of a group of ardent young aviators. D'Annunzio seemed glad to have escaped from women into his airplane. When I mentioned this to Richard, he started reminiscing about his own father's days as a pilot during World War I.

"It was the only time he was happy," Richard said, "the only time he was free of my mother." He had told me this before, but this time he connected it with his father's temper and then with his own tempers with Michael. The way he accepted his rages as inevitable infuriated me. But as usual I swallowed my anger and kept on with my efforts to placate him. The odd thing was that he hardly responded. He had a way of making me feel alone even when he was in the same room, and he was mostly out working.

Marooned with only the children as companions, I was desperately lonely. Not just for friendship. The idea of doing my Blake project with Estelle, the thought of having such a generous person to work with, kept me going. I wrote her every so often to tell her of my progress through Blake's prophetic books. Then one day Estelle wrote to me that seeing how well I'd done with my Yeats book—which I'd sent her—had inspired her to write her own book on Blake.

I couldn't believe it. I wrote her a measured letter suggesting we join forces and do the book together as coauthors, "sharing the glory." She wrote back a simple, "No."

I consoled myself by studying the permutations of Blake's rage, first against his brother, then his patronizing patron, then all the figures in his world that refused to recognize his genius. "It helps me forget my own anger," I wrote Maenchen, needing to tell someone. In retrospect, I was throwing out lifelines. Maenchen's reply about the benefits of sublimation didn't make me feel any better.

I was so lonely for female company that I started spending too much time with our maid, Mariella. Mariella was short and stocky with full breasts, very white skin and black hair tumbling around a broad, mobile face. She dressed sloppily, scuffing around in slippers, her skirt zipper partway down. She had come with the apartment, a palazzo on historic Via Giulia that I'd rented from a White Russian princess discovered by my mother. Mariella was full of energy and seeming goodwill. She oohed and ahhed over me as though I were a movie star, putting her hands around my waist, exclaiming about how small it was, telling me I looked beautiful in my clothes. When I caught a cold, she made me soothing drinks with honey. She sat with me in the kitchen and told me outrageous stories about the princess and how she slept with her dogs. Undoubtedly this should have warned me about her, and if I hadn't felt so needy, I might have resisted her invitations to swap stories.

Then one morning I came back from the archive and found Mariella holding Becca in her arms and showing her rings. Becca loved jewelry and was getting more and more excited as Mariella whispered to her that she was going to bring her a diamond or maybe an emerald. Then Mariella started swinging her to and fro and finally gave her a love bite on the arm that changed Becca's squeals into howls.

"What are you doing?" I asked, grabbing Becca from Mariella's arms and soothing her. "You're acting like an animal." *L'Animale* became Mariella's nickname. Once she brought a baby chick home for Michael for Easter and put it between her breasts. There was something almost bestial about her.

It was as though all the unspoken sexual tensions in our marriage were suddenly erupting. As though the nighttime secrets were parading through our apartment.

She referred to Richard respectfully as *il professore,* but I detected a slight hint of scorn in her voice. Once he reported to me that she rubbed by him in the hall with a *"Ciao, bello"* (Hi there, handsome). Another time we came home from the theater when she was babysitting to find her sprawled in a chair with her legs spread suggestively.

She started getting calls at the apartment. Always from "cousins" or her fiancé, the one who gave her the big ring on her finger. Later, from gossip at the Campo di Fiori market, I deduced that she was a *putana,* a whore, on the side.

I'm sure the children sensed something. Lisa was beginning to be interested in boys. She went to her first dance and came home to tell me how nice dancing felt. "Why do they say sex is bad," she asked me innocently, "when it feels so good to be close?" I felt a wave of panic. I'd had to work hard not to think about my own sexual frustration. With a nubile daughter in the house, it was going to be impossible.

Then we started having trouble with the water. There was only a limited supply for each household, held in big tanks on the roof. Suddenly there wasn't enough for the children to have their baths in the evening. It had mysteriously vanished. Lisa confided to me that she had seen Mariella washing the rags she used for her periods in the tub. I wanted to tell her to buy some pads. But instead I spoke to her about the necessity for conserving water. She started retreating into her room for hours, and I'd think I'd hear the water running in her sink. I became so preoccupied with her using up our water that I took Michael's periscope and tried to peer into her window from my own bedroom window. I was clearly going a bit batty.

Finally one night when I was arguing with her in the kitchen, Richard stalked in and gave an ultimatum. "One of you has to go." I fired her. The next day, she brought in the local priest, who accused us of mistreating a poor country girl and cheating her out of her benefits. She had specifically asked us not to subtract them since she wanted the higher pay, but now she sued us and won. All the anger I hadn't allowed myself to express for so long was directed at this woman with the flat face and darting black eyes. And the worst thing was that after she left we still didn't have enough water.

The Mariella episode scared me. It was too bizarre. I'd never been that far out of control before. A lot of feelings had gotten going that I didn't know I had. I came back from Rome with the conviction that something had to change. My first idea was to apply to the Psychoanalytic Institute again. It was probably an effort to find some sort of replacement for Estelle. I told myself that they hadn't admitted me the first time because I had only a book project. Now I was on my way to finishing a second book.

At my first interview, with Victor Calef, I tried hard to tell him what I'd discovered about Blake's misogyny and the—to me surprising—misogyny of the mostly male critics who dominated the Blake industry. Victor listened politely for a minute, then began to question me intently about my children. I couldn't get him onto my work. It seemed as though a person could be seen either as a patient or a potential colleague, and the analysts had shown me where they thought I belonged.

It's probably good I didn't get into the Institute. One of the requirements for training was another full analysis. And since change of situation was usually discouraged in an analysis, I probably never would have left my marriage. I think I kept returning to Maenchen in last-ditch attempts to keep married, to do my duty, as it were.

And if I had been trained as an analyst, I would have continually had to reckon with Maenchen. She was not only one of the senior analysts at the Institute, she was a training analyst. If they were really not going to admit me, I was free—or freer—of the burden of trying to meet her expectations.

"You are glad that I am letting you go," Maenchen said, when I left therapy again a year or so later, "because you see me as your superego and you want to be free to follow your impulses." This time she was right. I'd begun associating her with Blake's Urizen, his gray-haired rational God who crushes spontaneous joy. I found myself rooting for Urizen's opponent, Orc, the sexual liberator.

Chapter

13

*If I understood him well, he would have wanted
a woman who finally loved him enough to refuse
him. But it causes a woman discomfort not to
give herself.* —COLETTE

The day when my life really started to change was a Friday in
March 1978, when Richard left for Rome without me. For the first
time, I'd decided not to go with him on a research trip. Lisa was in
high school now—a demanding Berkeley prep school—and I didn't
want to disrupt her year. The tension in our marriage was hard
enough for her to handle. Michael, too, was showing signs of strain
and was seeing a therapist, a man analyzed by Maenchen, who
through two years of treatment failed to pick up the fact that
Michael had been abused by his male teacher. It was another case of
concentrating on inner dynamics when there was something glaring-
ly wrong outside.

It was the first time in my marriage that I had been separated
from Richard and I was astonished at how good it felt. Life with the
children seemed easier and I was finishing the final draft of my
Blake book. Then as in any good romance, I met a dark, handsome
stranger. It was at a party given by an older woman friend, Isabel
Stampp, a faculty wife who used to invite Richard and me over as a
couple but stopped because she hated the way Richard put me down
in public. I think now that she put me next to Will at the table that
April actually hoping that something would come of it. He was a
high-power lawyer, a former radical and, most significant, separated from his wife. He was also worried about his daughter growing
up in the too-fast world of 1970s Berkeley. He wanted to take her
away to Italy for a semester and divert her mind from rock-and-roll

to art and culture. His puritanical zeal to protect his daughter intrigued me. It must have reminded me of my father. I said I'd try to find out about a school for her. We agreed to have lunch.

Sitting together at a Chinese restaurant, very much the helpful matron, I gave him the name of the best school in Florence and the telephone number of someone who might have a villa. Then he asked me about my work. I was thinking about Blake's *Marriage of Heaven and Hell*, I told him, about Blake's fear of impulse. "Oh," Will said, raising his eyebrows. Our conversation would have made a good scene in a Woody Allen comedy, where characters always discuss their neurotic fears before acting them out. Will got the point and immediately started asking me about my marriage. He thought, Will said, batting his luxuriously thick eyelashes, that some people married because they were afraid of letting themselves go.

If someone had said "Let's show this woman what she is missing in life," she would have invented Will. He was the type of man who can sense a woman's needs and make just the gestures to gratify them. He fed me complicated dishes, bought me clothes, read poetry to me, and most astonishing—since he was someone with an important job of his own—spent hours reading my Blake manuscript, thinking of ways of expanding it or making it clearer. Though he was having trouble with some writing of his own at the time, he seemed to be wholeheartedly wishing for my success, wanting the publisher to turn somersaults when he saw the book. Estelle had immersed herself in my work, but this was the first time I'd had this gratification from a male friend.

I think I would have been content to keep Will as a platonic friend even though I was wildly attracted to him. I was infatuated, but I was also frightened. He'd been married twice, was still not divorced, and had recently broken off with a long-term mistress. Besides this, he had had scores of other relationships, many of them during his marriage. By his own description he started off each affair with great expectations, and ended disillusioned. Women always disappointed him. Not a good bet.

Maybe it was my fears that drove me to confide in my neighbors, Nick and Alice Govotnik. They were a striking-looking couple who lived very privately in a Craftsman house high on a hill on the next block. They had been married for years and still spent a lot of time walking hand in hand, pointedly lovers. Nick was a specialist in

160

Dostoyevski and translated literary pornography on the side. Alice was a poet. I had given Nick chapters of my Blake manuscript to read, but my main relationship with them was through Becca. They had no children and acted as unofficial godparents. On her birthday they would get up before dawn to string balloons and poems on the bushes; they encouraged her paintings and poems, and had a special dress-up box that transformed Alice into Mother Goose and Nick into a character called Froggie. For a child, their house was a heaven of make-believe.

In other ways they were like characters from before the Russian Revolution. They dressed elegantly for dinner every night. She in a long gown, he in a velvet smoking jacket. Sometimes Alice wore more risqué outfits and put on what she referred to as "shows" for Nick. She was always perfectly coiffed and dressed, wearing her makeup even at night because she didn't want to break the illusion.

They were in fact masters of illusion. Alice had been an officer in the Marines, but because Nick didn't like to see her in rough clothes, she did her gardening work only when he was out and, by the time he came back, was demurely seated by the fireside in her long gown.

Their house with its fairy garden and center chimney was a perfect laboratory for imaginative acts, and on impulse one night I told them about my early encounters with Will. With Richard away, I was overexcited and lonely. There were glowing lights in their window. They were infinitely charming and interested. I sipped my wine and laughingly told them about a story I was thinking of writing about a difficult marriage. I saw them exchange glances. Why write one, their glances said, when here was an opportunity to actually live a drama.

Gradually the Govotniks took on the role of codirectors of my meetings with Will. I was the ingenue, the good mother. Will became cast as the seducer. Through their eyes I began to realize how naïve and limited they thought I was, or at least how vague and sweet. This may have been the first time I really saw what I looked like from outside.

What seemed to intrigue them was the idea that my mixture of vague sweetness and hidden brains would somehow defeat the seducer. We all agreed that Will was the kind of man who would lose interest in a woman the minute he had her. We'd beat him at his own game. Nick lent me Kierkegaard's *Diary of a Seducer,* in which a man consciously destroys all of a woman's restraints one by one and then abandons her. We thought about it together, shivering deliciously, and then Alice and Nick suggested a counterstrategy. The main action was a holding one, delay. I can't remember what we thought would happen eventually. Was Will supposed to come to love me, really love me, and then it would be all right? Or was I to delay indefinitely? I don't know. All I know is that I resisted for six months with the most gratifying results.

Will heaped intensity on intensity to win me. He wrote me every day describing his love; he bought me expensive champagne and insisted on drinking some out of my slipper. He showed me myself in his mirror in a variety of colors and textures, picking out what made me look best—doing what mothers often do with their daughters.

And through it all, I reported the events, recast almost ready for fiction, to the Govotniks. They reacted to them the way people would to readings of Dickens around the fire. They'd ask for favorite parts over again—when he cried over our gourmet lunch because I was married, and when he said he wanted to be more than a lover, he wanted to be a husband. I wonder why he keeps saying that, they would ask each other, and why he talks so much about the children. Why can't he just let it be between him and Brenda. Maybe he really wants a family, I'd say, and they'd shake their heads. This wasn't how they saw the drama going.

Alice and Nick were as fascinated by Will as I was. They watched him on television when he had an appearance one day. They loved his style, the way he dressed, the way he talked. They saw I was scared, but they wanted to keep me going. The whole thing was fun for them. Every couple of nights, I'd come over and sit with them while they had their martinis, watching the sun setting over the bay, and I'd tell them the latest installment. Acting as if it were all a play made it seem safer for me—it gave me the illusion that I—my team—was in control.

After Richard came home from his three months in Italy, Nick had a moment of compunction. Maybe you don't want to go ahead with this, he said. Richard had come back and announced that he had decided our marriage was "worth it." Worth the heartache it had given him. I'm sure he meant it, but it just made me mad. How could he declare that from above, as it were? Worth it to whom and how? I told him I had met a man who liked me and whom I wanted to keep seeing. He knew Will and made a few disparaging comments. Tell him your husband doesn't want you to see him, he said, as though he hadn't heard what I said or as if the matter were simply one between men. We didn't speak about it again.

Richard had gone away in the spring. By the next fall, I still hadn't slept with Will, though we'd had several stormy partings and reunions. He was going away for the spring semester as he'd planned, taking his teenage daughter to Florence. I felt as if he were a soldier going off to war. I wanted to make sure of him and give him something to remember me by. He had insisted until then that I be in absolute agreement in our lovemaking (we were kissing by then). I would much rather have been swept away. But one day, when we'd been sitting in the rose garden while he slowly stroked my arm, and bees buzzed in overblown flowers, I simply asked him to take me home.

I half expected it to be all over after that, but it wasn't. Worse, I found myself passionately in love. Alice and Nick thought he'd fallen in love too this time, that I'd been different enough from what he was used to, to confuse and seduce him in his turn. But they warned me to be careful—any hint of possessiveness and they thought he'd be off. Will was like some exotic bird who had to keep migrating, Alice said. He needed his freedom. She told me how she'd always given Nick the sense of an open door so he could fly away. They could see I wanted to clutch and hold Will, but I wouldn't be able to keep him unless I backed off.

Before Will left for Italy, I arranged to meet him in New York on a visit to see my mother, who had been having some bad falls, apparently caused by hardening of the arteries. We stayed at the Stanhope in a glorious old-fashioned room a few blocks from 1192 Park Avenue. After a visit to the Met, to see the Tutankhamen exhibit, I took him over there to meet Mother. He was enchanted with her, kissed her hand, was incredibly gallant. But after I got home, she called me and told me that I should watch out. He was weak, she said, and she was afraid he'd drag me down. When I questioned her, she said she had been a Don Juan too in her youth. She knew the signs, the insatiability for love. She was very worried. I wasn't in a mood to listen to her advice.

By the time Will left for his semester in Italy, I was writing him the same overheated letters he was writing me—though mine were lighter on adjectives. Perhaps I should have worried at the way he compared his love to the Taj Mahal and other sacred or monumental objects. As I had learned from Yeats, nothing brings out the itch to degrade more than a queen on a pedestal.

Will wrote me almost every day until he came back in May of 1979, addressing letters to me at Alice and Nick's as B. Govotnik. After I read each letter I would give them bits of news. He is discovering the Baroque, living next to an opera singer, visiting the charming *pensione* you told him about.

We had a joyful reunion in the summer—Alice and Nick joined us for an Italian dinner in the city. I wore a 1930s black dress that he'd found for me, decorated with rhinestone clips, and slung my fur stole over my shoulder. He wore what I thought of as his mafioso suit, gray-striped with a soft fedora. Though he kept saying he wanted me to divorce by my next birthday, it seemed as if we could just go on this way forever. Since Richard was so oblivious, we even began to include the children on some of our outings, taking Becca for ice cream or to the park, taking all of them bowling—Will was a super bowler. I probably shouldn't have involved them, but I had an urge to share my happiness. Even more, I loved the illusion of a family doing things together. Will's interest in them was irresistible.

Then suddenly Will's father died and things began to unravel. He became morose and I couldn't seem to help him. He would lie curled on his bed next to a picture of his father and him playing tennis when he was a child, and think about how he hadn't ever completed the work he'd been planning to do.

When his mother came to visit, things got worse. She wore designer eyeglasses and worried a lot about the stock market. On the few occasions he invited me over when she was there, we didn't hit it off. Together they looked through old scrapbooks. He showed me a picture of his first wife, a curvy brunette in a white dress. Her father had been really nice to him. "I let him down," he said gloomily.

Alice and Nick suggested soothing hugs. Just tell him you understand, they said. But I didn't really. I only knew that he was slipping away.

Troubled, I actually went back to Maenchen for a few sessions. I think I expected her to play my conscience. But she surprised me by seeing Will as the love of my life. When I told her he was a lawyer like my father, she almost purred. As I described him, he seemed full of care for me and for my children. She was particularly impressed that he invited Becca for tea. Maenchen thought he was depressed by his father's death. And maybe by the fact that I wouldn't commit myself to him. We should analyze why I felt I needed two men. Why I couldn't let one go.

I tried to explain that there was no evidence Will could have a committed relationship with anyone, that he had a reputation as a Don Juan. Even his therapist despaired of him. Once when I had broken up with him for a few days, the therapist in an unguarded moment told a friend of mine, who was also in therapy with him, that I was lucky to be out of it, that Will would never give himself to a woman.

"Every relationship is different," Maenchen said. "Your father was engaged eight times, but he had a committed relation with your mother. I don't see why you can't ask Richard for a trial separation to see how things work out with Will."

In a somewhat pathetic attempt to see what it would feel like to be married to Will, I bought him some bath towels—his were old and raveling at the sides. He hated the new ones and felt I wanted to imprison him like a bug in amber.

"He didn't ask you to act as his wife, did he?" Maenchen grumbled. "Why do you do these things?"

"I guess I misunderstood . . ."

"A man–woman thing isn't necessarily a marriage," she said.

A month later, I asked Richard for a separation. By now, I half believed that Will really could be a different person with me if I wasn't so suspicious of his every move. Both Maenchen and the Govotniks told me to give him space. Maenchen, though, didn't want to think about his trickster aspects. She seemed to think he was sincere. He might not want marriage, but he loved me, wanted to be with me. I had to give him a chance to prove it.

Richard was devastated by the idea of a separation and tried to frighten me by saying it had to be a divorce or nothing. He begged me not to do it. He had been unfaithful too, he said, so he didn't care about what I'd done—I could commit adultery a thousand times and he'd still want me. He was relieved, in fact, because it made him feel less guilty about what he'd been doing.

All in a rush he told me how he'd discovered sex, how my sexuality was what first attracted him to me, how fucking was everything to him.

Now it seems sad that this was the fullest conversation we ever had. Thinking about it now, I believe that he loved me and had managed to convince himself that his casual encounters had no relevance to our marriage. But then I was simply in a state of shock. No little bell rang in my head making sense of everything. It was all simply unimaginable. Totally confusing. I'd lived with a man for almost twenty years and I didn't know him, not at all. There was no way I could stay with him now.

After I finished crying in Will's arms, he told me he didn't want to be named as a co-respondent. We'd better cool things for a while and let my marriage die a natural death. We shouldn't sleep together anymore. Though I was sad, I accepted it as something temporary.

There was a lot to do. Richard had to find a place. I said I'd help him. And I decided to take a part-time job teaching fourth grade at Becca's school in Oakland. I wasn't going to ask for alimony since I had some money of my own, but I thought it wouldn't hurt to supplement it by working. Will said I could come over to his house every day to do my lesson plans and correct homework. He kept telling me it was wonderful the way I was turning my life around, but the way he said it made me feel he was talking over my coffin.

Maenchen didn't believe me when I told her Will was withdrawing.

"But you just told me how he calls you and talks to you about each of your children in turn. That doesn't sound as if he's going to break it off."

And it was true he kept up his interest in the children.

Then suddenly in late October 1979, I got a call from my brother telling me Mother had made another suicide attempt.

"I found her lying in the hall," he said, "covered with vomit."

"Where is she now?"

"In intensive care. She took a mixture of painkillers and sleeping pills. They're not sure if she'll wake up . . ."

I didn't go right away, thinking rather heartlessly that if she was asleep, my presence wouldn't make much difference. But a few days later Chris told me he was thinking of telling the doctors to disconnect her from life support. He was afraid if she did wake up, she'd be a vegetable.

"Wait till I get there," I said. "I want to have a look at her myself."

Maenchen told me it was going to be a terrible shock seeing her hooked up to all the machines. She obviously didn't think I could cope, but I was beginning to find a new center of strength.

I sat by Mother's bed in intensive care and talked to her for hours, told her what I was doing and how I'd left Richard, but mostly I told her how I wanted her to come back, how she just had to live. Eventually, when my voice was about to give out, her eyelids fluttered and she opened her eyes and looked at me. The nurses couldn't believe it. But there she was, and in a sense something was healed. I got to replay that awful day when I was fifteen and found her in her room asleep. Then I'd felt completely helpless, frightened out of my mind. This time, I wasn't afraid for myself or horrified at what she'd done. I wasn't even mad at her. When she woke up, I felt it as a personal triumph. She'd heard me calling her and answered. When she could eat a little, I fed her Jell-O, spoon by spoon.

When I got back to Berkeley, Will took me out for my birthday—I was forty-three—and we broke the rule against making love. That night, going back to his house to pick up something I'd forgotten, I found him with another woman, a flaming redhead. We had a screaming battle the next day in which he told me he'd never marry me. How could he trust the judgment of a woman who hadn't known the sort of man she was married to. Besides, if my husband did the things I said he did, he, Will, could have picked up a venereal disease from me. Had I thought of that? His therapist—ironically, the one I'd persuaded him to see and who'd said he was hopeless—had told him my life sounded like a snakepit, and he wanted out. Later he apologized for his bluntness, and kept calling once a week for the next six months, but my idyll was over.

Maenchen thought the only possibility for getting Will back was self-control, no blame, an appearance of calm. Just what she had always advised with Richard. When I broke down one night and went to Will's house, probably wanting to strangle the other woman, Maenchen shook her head over me.

"Now you've lost him for good," she said. Instead of lecturing me, she might have pointed out that even if I got him back he'd bring me nothing but heartache. But she just gave her long-suffering sigh.

When I had a dream of jumping off a roof, she suggested I take a rest in an institution where I could get medication. That made me mad. Did she really think I'd leave my children and go off to the loony bin? Instead, I told Will what a louse he was, how he'd led me on, saying how much he wanted to marry me—and then simply walked away, saying, "See you around." I told him I didn't want him calling anymore. He could take his mercy mission elsewhere.

Chapter

14

~

We live in a period when the demands of the
roles defined by the sex-gender system have
created widespread discomfort and resistance. . . .
The elimination of the present organization of
parenting in favor of a system of parenting in
which both men and women are responsible
would be a tremendous social advance.
                                    —NANCY CHODOROW

About a year later, in the spring of 1981, I was sitting in my
newly renovated study—it had been Richard's and had a command-
ing view of the ocean and Mount Tamalpais—having my weekly
conversation with my mother. Richard's books had all been crated
up and given to him and mine were lining the newly painted shelves.
The curtains he'd let the cat tear into tatters were down and I had a
champagne-colored wool carpet and a new woven-grass shade that
smelled like freshly mown hay. It was my first private workspace;
up till then, I'd worked in a corner of our bedroom. Best of all, I had
a letter from my editor at Macmillan on my desk saying that the
English edition of my Yeats book had done quite decently, reviews
had been generally good, and, if they were available, Macmillan
wanted world rights to my Blake book. The book would be sure to
ruffle some feathers, he said, but that was fine with him. It was an
original work. He liked it. They were going to publish it with sixty
illustrations from Blake's *Songs* and the prophetic books. Besides
that, two anthologies of critical method were taking excerpts from
my Yeats book. In one, I was sandwiched between Harold Bloom
and Jacques Derrida as an example of criticism based on psychoanalytic object relations. Not bad for someone who never went to conferences or gave lectures or even had a job.

When I told her, Mother sounded really happy for me—though I
knew she thought I sometimes overinterpreted Blake's texts—and I

decided this was as good a time as any to tell her about my new friend Ira.

"Mother," I said cautiously into my new white phone, "I'm going out with someone really special." When she didn't say anything, I went on in a rush. "He's in the history department. He writes about Islam. I've already read his book. I like the way he thinks. But what I really like is, Mom, we're having so much fun. We go to the races. We laugh all the time. I think the children like him too. I want you to meet him."

I'd seen Ira at parties for twenty years, first with his wife and then alone, and though I had waited to tell Mother about it, we'd already been going out for months. When Ira went to New York that summer, he visited my mother.

"She was the most aloof person I'd ever met," he told me later. "A bit like Queen Victoria. It wasn't that she wasn't gracious. She was. She brought up subjects, mostly about art, and we discussed them, but there was no warmth, no suggestion that she was talking to a prospective son-in-law."

Going out with Ira was fun. It was also deeply satisfying. On one of our first dates he made salmon on his hibachi. "I can imagine cooking meals for you the rest of my life," he told me. He took me to serious theater and romantic movies and everywhere we held hands. When we went to the track, I climbed the fence screaming encouragement to my chosen horse. Someone else might have been embarrassed. "I've never seen anyone get so excited," he said. "I love it, the joy you get out of ordinary things. You just have to learn to relax a little and you'll be perfect." Then he laughed because he was as high-strung as I was.

Like me, Ira wanted a life that balanced work and pleasure. But there were difficulties too. We each had our separate children to care about: his only child, Alex, was fifteen, and although Lisa was away at Wesleyan, Becca and Michael were still at home and going to school in Berkeley. Everyone was suffering the seismic effects of the breakup. "If you could stand living with Dad for twenty years," Becca said accusingly, "why couldn't you stand it for twenty more?"

"Maybe relationships take work to keep going," Michael suggested, precociously wise. But he was upset about Ira. When he asked me what I thought it felt like having "a man" sleeping with your mother, I flushed to the roots of my hair. If Ira and I hadn't both felt that this was the love we'd been waiting for, our last chance to be happy, we might not have been able to stick out the three years before we married.

When my anxiety level became too high, I went back to Maenchen yet again. Like a battered wife who can't stay away from her abusive husband, I told myself that this time it would be different; she'd really help me. Ira and I could have really used some good practical advice on how to talk to each other and our children. Instead, my analyst gave me her usual suggestions: control yourself, show restraint, don't exhibit any anger. Once I reported that I gave Ira a shove when he took my place on the sofa and Maenchen said, "That's not a female thing to do."

"Ideas about women have changed," I told her. "Don't you know that?" To my surprise she said that maybe I was right. If I'd started standing up to her consistently, probably she would have backed down. But I was still under a more powerful spell than that of any old-time witch. Especially powerful because I was unaware of it. I mistakenly thought that because I never "loved" her, I wasn't tied to her. Later, an analyst friend told me that a negative transference is stronger than a positive one and that it doesn't vanish when you stop therapy for a few years. It exerts a pull on you until you have confronted it. In any case, because of my emotional dependence I could no more see that she was beating up on me than an abused wife can see abuse. I convinced myself that, though she made mistakes, she was helping me face reality. At the same time, I had a suspicion that her reality wasn't necessarily mine.

Since I couldn't escape the force field of the transference, I took a detour. It was much easier to knock her sister witches off their pedestals. I got the idea of writing about the early women analysts in Freud's circle.

A friend, Marilyn Fabe, wanted to collaborate with me. She thought we should call our book *What Do Women Want?* I proposed starting with Helene Deutsch, Mother's analyst in the 1920s in Vienna. Not only would this give me a chance to see what Deutsch thought about being female—she was famous for her emphasis on female masochism—but it would enable me to learn more about my mother. I had a similarly personal interest in Muriel

Gardiner and in Ruth Mack Brunswick. Phyllis Greenacre was the only analyst I wanted to include who hadn't been part of my parents' life, and I picked her because she had written extensively about artists and writers, and she was considered one of the mothers of psychoanalysis.

My task, as I saw it, was a friendly one. Being accused of hostility is still something that induces rapid, head-shaking denial. Many feminists were very down on analysis. I was going to find redeeming qualities in the women analysts (just the way I hoped to find Maenchen helpful) and then explain them to the feminists. If I'd realized that I really wanted to bring the whole analytic establishment crashing down so that Maenchen's couch would be buried in the rubble, I probably wouldn't have been able to begin.

I started with Helene Deutsch and was pleasantly surprised to find that she really wasn't as negative as she seemed to the feminists. Though Deutsch paid lip service to Freud's idea that women are masochistic, passive enviers, her case histories show her urging her women patients to fight masochistic tendencies by finding and sustaining meaningful work.

Before I drafted my article, I interviewed Mother about her analysis with Deutsch. Mother's fragile health gave a sense of urgency to our conversation. Besides, this was the "faith" we had both lived in. And even though the promised "cure" never came, Mother still spoke about Dr. Kris as if she were God.

The interview started slowly. Mother had been reluctant to talk to me, insisting that she didn't have much to tell. Then suddenly Mother confessed that Deutsch had "brutally" thrown her out after two years. Some people just didn't come across, Deutsch said, and Mother was one of them.

After this, our conversation heated up rapidly. Mother began to talk about her problem with "sadism." Now, I thought, finally I'd get to hear her secrets instead of always telling her mine. She'd tormented men, Mother went on in her aristocratic voice. She had been treated with great sadism by her brother and this was her revenge. The philosopher Mortimer Adler was in love with her in her twenties. She saw a lot of him because she endlessly admired his brilliance. He was teaching in the honors course at Columbia, she said, "and he made me read everything his students read. He wouldn't give a lecture until he had come to talk with me.

"I was kept abreast of everything and he was utterly brilliant. But then he started to try to make love to me and he was all bones. I never saw anyone with so many bones. Wherever he touched you was a bone. I tried to de-bonify him," she said with a certain co-quettishness, "to teach him to be softer, but it was just impossible, that side of the thing was a total failure." She raised her thin shoulders expressively. "This was the point where Deutsch pointed out to me that I was being sadistic."

She seemed to get pleasure from remembering this. "I called him Suzy," her voice dropped to a conspiratorial whisper, "and Dr. Deutsch thought that was dreadful." At this I heard myself laughing, excited against my will by this relation of my mother's powers. And of course I knew she could be cruel, though my analysts never discussed it with me, and I had trouble admitting it, just as I had trouble admitting Richard's cruelty or Maenchen's. It seemed natural, what people who "cared" for you did.

But hearing this had the effect of slipping another little piece of my own puzzle in place. I began to see how the first relationship set the pattern for the next. How by expecting a certain kind of treatment, I unwittingly invited it.

Even at eighty, Mother could still make me feel like a helpless child. Remembering herself as a young woman, her eyes bored through me like a hawk's. I thought I knew how poor awkward Mortimer had felt trying to caress her, catching sight of those eyes.

While I was looking at her, suddenly the fierceness went out of her eyes and the eyelids lowered demurely.

"Deutsch really did help me a great deal," she said. "That was the end of my being sadistic, and soon after I left her, I got married to your father. I didn't have that in me anymore." She bowed her head, hiding herself still further. "Except very slightly."

About this time, my friend Marilyn got pregnant and abandoned our project of writing about the women analysts. Undeterred, I decided to go ahead with the individual pieces that interested me most. I met Nancy Chodorow, who was beginning her work on the influence of women analysts on the development of psychoanalysis, and our discussions reinforced my wish to bridge the gap between analysts and feminists. After my Deutsch essay appeared in *Signs: Journal of Women in Culture and Society*, feminist women who had dismissed Deutsch told me they had gone back to take another look. Someone even phoned me and asked, "Is this Brenda Webster, the feminist?"

"Yes," I said after a moment's thought. "I guess it is."

I went back East and interviewed both Muriel Gardiner and Phyllis Greenacre. Muriel met me in the living room of our old house at the farm. She had donated the farm to the Stony Brook Millstone Watershed Association and the house had become the headquarters of a park. Trails crisscrossed the fields and pastures, trooped over by locals and kids from the city.

Muriel still lived in a small house on the property. She was her usual indomitable self; though her deeply tanned face was cracked like old leather, her voice was vibrant. I was struck again by what a rare person she was, a free spirit. She'd never believed that women were innately masochistic, or passive, or envious. She dared to write a paper in the 1930s making fun of the sheeplike behavior of analysts' wives. Laughing, she told me how her colleagues were always telling her she needed re-analysis. And in her old age, still actively pursuing unpopular causes, she'd written an empathetic, wise book, *The Deadly Innocents: Portraits of Children Who Kill,* about children pushed beyond endurance who kill their parents. She'd even taken one of them into her home after he got out of jail. He was coming along well, she told me, taking care of lab animals. He had learned not to introduce himself by saying, "Hello, I'm John; I killed my mother with an ax."

After Muriel's forthrightness and warmth, Phyllis Greenacre struck me as an exceedingly closed person. "Psychoanalysis was a cloak for my shyness," she told me at one point. "I was terribly, pathologically, shy." She usually refused interviews—she hadn't let Nancy Chodorow interview her—and only let me come because of our shared interest in Blake. She had originally wanted to go into literary studies, she told me, but hadn't been recognized as one of the promising students in college.

She had a large apartment in the Nineties with windows that looked out on the East River. Her connection to psychoanalysis, like that of many early analysts, had started in her teens when she read Freud's *Three Contributions to the Theory of Sex.* When I asked her what she thought when she first came across Freud's theory of women, she said she didn't really pay it that much attention.

When I pressed her, she said, in a rather patronizing way that reminded me of Maenchen, that people got too upset over theory. They reified the concepts, which were really were quite flexible and in process of development.

If this was true, I asked her, why were there so few advances in theory about women from within the movement? She looked out the window at the view. Freud always admitted there were things he didn't know, she said, but though the social situation did have an effect on women's development, basically the difference was anatomical. To illustrate, she told me how her daughter would rush up to see her baby brother when his diaper was being changed and make comments about not having a penis, saying, "Peter is lost," or "Where is Peter?"

"People make altogether too much fuss over the statement 'biology is destiny,'" she said. "Sure it is, but it's not something to get so upset about."

I was curious what Eissler would think about all this and asked if I could interview him. I hadn't seen him for years though we'd corresponded, and I was astonished to see how vulnerable he looked, his gray hair, his austere eyeglasses with their metal rims contrasting with his sensual lips. He said he knew the feminists didn't like him but felt it was unfair. It was not so easy to be a man. A man always had to face possible rejection. I asked him whether he still thought only men could be geniuses. Yes, he said. Because it's based on a very simple biological fact. Men produce an unlimited quantity of sperm in their lifetimes, women a limited quantity of eggs. "But women can be exquisitely talented," he added, with European courtliness, "like yourself, and think how difficult it is for the man who knows he could be a genius—and isn't."

I tried gently to point out to him that he was being even more biologically minded than Freud, but Eissler wouldn't budge.

Like Greenacre, Eissler was a believer in phallic power. I'd hoped that, as I had with Deutsch, I'd find a split between her theory and her practice, but I'd been disappointed. Not only did she take Freud's ideas about penis envy to heart, she went one better. She invented the concept of penis awe and glowingly described her female patients' visions of penises flashing halos of colored lights. All hail the Penis-God!

When I was at her apartment, she told me briefly about a patient who, according to Greenacre's bizarre interpretation, thought she was a penis: she held her body like this, Greenacre told me, straightening her shoulders and adding another inch to her short stature. You see, erect. If I hadn't known Greenacre was a famous psychoanalyst I might have thought I was talking to an inmate at a mental hospital.

Rereading Greenacre's work, I wanted to rescue her from her own excesses. These surreal interpretations of hers coexisted with work that seemed to contradict them. Her studies of fetishists, in particular, seemed to me to open the way to a reinterpretation of women's penis envy. According to Freud, fetishists—like other men but in a more extreme fashion—are horrified by the castrated female genitals and fear a similar loss. This is why they need a symbolic extra penis, a fetish, to reassure them before they can have sex. Greenacre argues that this is all wrong. They aren't afraid of losing their penises; they actually don't have a sense of having them. Their problem, she suggests, is that because of traumatic early handling they can't outgrow their primary identification with their mothers. These men are like the Woody Allen hero who jokes that he's the only man he knows with penis envy; they need the fetish to give them a sense of having the right male equipment.

This implicitly challenged Freud's view of the centrality of men, but I wanted Greenacre to go one step further. I wanted her to say that if a grown woman still wants a penis, it is probably a result of similar early trauma that damaged her sense of her own genitals rather than, as Freud suggested, an inescapable envy of the male's superior organ.

Greenacre disappointed me. She wouldn't admit that most adult women accept and like their genitals. She had case evidence that a girl's envy was increased by parental preference for a brother, but she kept insisting envy was innate. To make matters worse, she wrote a paper on female sexuality that made Eissler's assumptions look pale. She said, for instance, that women would never be comfortable with their sexuality because they had two different—and confusing—sexual zones, a vagina and a clitoris, and that women artists couldn't externalize their work as well as males because they lacked an external organ.

It may sound ridiculous now, but this woman was and still is considered a major psychoanalytic theorist. She wrote beautiful prose and had a clear lucid argumentative style that gave new force to concepts I thought I'd outgrown. I was overawed by her, much as I think she was by Freud. When her insights varied from Freud's, she squashed them before they had a chance to develop. She couldn't let herself contradict him for more than a few pages. The same thing was happening to me.

When I told Maenchen that I was stuck, she said that my exploring psychoanalytic concepts only made me more anxious. I should concentrate on my problems.

But what if the concepts themselves were part of what was making me anxious, I asked her. It wasn't reassuring to read, for example, compelling explanations of why women artists need imaginary penises, or why they can't be good mothers.

"No one is making you read it," she said; "you are choosing this disturbance for yourself."

But that wasn't the point. Theory not only reflected the power relations in the Victorian family and the way I had lived my life, but it also underlay Maenchen's treatment of me. Thinking about her attitude, I began to suspect that these early women theorists—including Maenchen herself with her mountain-climbing bravado—thought of themselves as honorary men. The new field gave them an access to power, sometimes quite extraordinary power. But, as Nancy Chodorow also found when she interviewed them, it didn't make them feminists or even—except for Deutsch—particularly concerned with studying and understanding women.

No matter how much I tried, I couldn't finish my essay on Greenacre.

I started writing fiction again soon after I met Ira, late in 1979. We'd been walking in the woods one day and suddenly I said to him that I wanted to write some stories about my childhood, but I was afraid. I had spent so many years at this other sort of writing, could I really start all over again? He was wonderful. "Just do it," he told me, laughing. "Worry about it afterward." Once I started, the stories came pouring out, almost faster than I could get them down.

Meanwhile, Eissler sent me an article of his that bemoaned what can only be described as a loss of reverence for the penis. Instead of being an instrument of awe with monoliths constructed to it, it seemed to be taking on the status of a toy. Inspired by this odd nostalgia, I wrote a story called "The Ultimate Toy," in which an analyst named Lucretia decides she's had enough of Freudian theory and of her profession—she's going to be an artist. When she appears at a meeting of the New York Psychoanalytic Association to present a paper on penis envy, she announces instead that the concept is a lot of hot air and says she is going to offer something to replace it. While Lucretia is talking, Phyllis Greenacre's ghost—I happily imagined her dead—makes running derogatory comments.

Lucretia, unlike me with Maenchen, pays no attention. She motions to her assistant to bring over her action sculpture, the ultimate toy. It is a balloon-like appendage set between two spheres built on a wheeled base so it can be pulled along like a child's toy. The analysts in the audience immediately begin to make far-fetched interpretations of its meaning, quarrelling over whether it suggests the pre-Oedipal or the Oedipal period. Lucretia calmly deconstructs the toy. She detaches the inflated rubber stem, lets out some air and shows how it can be twisted and shaped into cuddly animals. It is also perfect for active play, she tells them, sending the balloon stem spinning, whistling into the audience. When it collapses, deflated, she hauls it back by its nylon string.

"*Fort-da, fort-da*," shouts a man from the back, "just like Freud's grandson with the spool of thread. Here, there, the action's the same. It's brilliant."

"You fool! Can't you see it's not the action that's important, it's the size change," another man sputters indignantly.

After demonstrating that the toy can also be unzipped and used as a raincoat, Lucretia tells her assistant to take orders, and while the analysts rush toward the podium she slips out the back door and heads for the airport.

Making fun of the theory of penis envy was liberating. Instead of feeling my hand and brain go limp, I could laugh. When I finished laughing, I decided I wasn't going to be an apologist for psychoanalysis anymore, or keep writing psychoanalytic critiques of male poets. I was going to write fiction. That was it. I had both the right work and the right love now.

My wedding to Ira took place outside in the garden in the fall of

1983. I had hung flowers under all the live oaks and there was a *chupah* covered with a prayer shawl and twined with peach-colored roses and narcissus. My best friend, Carol, was mopping her eyes as I walked down the path in my long white muslin dress. It was that kind of perfectly romantic occasion, the fairytale happy ending. Our respective children stood at each of the supporting poles of the *chupah*. Becca holding the rings, Michael the glass to be broken, Alex and Lisa looking slightly dazed. They were in their best clothes, and had put a pink ribbon around our dog Poppy's neck.

The rabbi told us some marriages were made in heaven. Ours clearly was. We kissed.

Unlike a true-romance story, our problems didn't melt away like snow in the heat of our love. But love kept us going. We struggled and swore and said we couldn't do it, then we tried harder. We even went to a marriage counsellor, Dr. Berg. I liked him so much I saw him for a while alone after our ten joint sessions were over. It was a revelation.

"It looks like you've spent a lot of wasted years in analysis," he told me. Berg had been traditionally trained, but had become disillusioned by the orthodox approach and become selectively eclectic. He didn't want to analyze my obsessions. He referred to them cheerfully as "space garbage."

"It doesn't really matter what the content is," he told me, with a wave of his hand. "It's an old pattern, that's all. You don't need it anymore. When you feel the thoughts coming, just toss them out." It was such a relief.

When I told him how bad I thought I was, citing Maenchen, he gave me his most mischievous smile. (Sometimes he would even give me an unorthodox hug.) He accepted me, liked me, wanted to help and did help simply by being a mensch. While he sat there finishing his tuna sandwich, I'd tell him what I thought I could do to make things better at home. He was so much my advocate that I'd end up defending Ira or my children or my mother and seeing their point of view. For the first time, I felt as if I had something to do with the process. In fact I was doing it. He was just the kindly observer. When he gave suggestions they were given in a way that engaged rather than repelled me. He got me not to blurt out the first thing that came to my mind by making me curious about what I'd learn if I were quiet—not by shaming me about my lack of control.

With Berg I discovered that I learned more about myself by writing stories than I had in years of therapy. I wrote the voices of my childhood, and when I read them I learned things. I experimented with making my characters change on paper before I ever changed in person. And what was wonderful about Berg was he got as excited about it as I did.

"I can't hear you," my mother said on our weekly phone call, "speak louder."

"I'm speaking as loud as I can," I yelled back. "Mom, can you hear me now?" After another series of bad falls, she'd taken to her bed and refused to get up. I was worried.

"A little."

"I'm going to visit you. I'll get the ticket today, all right?"

As I sat by her bed holding her hand, she lay there beaming at me. She started talking about *The Death of Socrates,* a painting she had done years before when she was imagining her own death. She had given Socrates a coverlet of flowers. "I think of myself like that, of living on in the colors, in the leaves," she gestured at the pots of violets she always kept near her bed, "of being spread around." She smiled as if it were a special joke between us.

"Then I'll get some of you too," I said. "I'm glad."

She was making a joke but was serious, too, in that elliptical way of hers. She was passing on her mantle, her creative gift. And though I had always hated the way she compared herself to Kierkegaard and Dante, I was touched. At least she wasn't still mad at me for trying to write, and it was wonderful how she managed to transcend her body as it disintegrated.

I sit beside her, feeding her Jell-O. She opens her mouth for it like a baby bird. A tube runs from under her covers into a bag filled with yellow fluid. "I never refuse an angel," she says, referring to a vision she's had.

"Have another spoonful," I say. "Was it the same angel this time?"

"It was many angels," she says, "and a turtle. Isn't that curious?"

"Yes," I say. "Have you had enough Jell-O? Do you want to drink?"

"I like you to feed me," she says, "but I'm not hungry anymore. Could you just hold the spoon there in my mouth?"

Mother's funeral in November 1984 was everything she would have wanted: the big hall was filled with banks of spring flowers; there was a quartet playing Bach; my brother and I read selections from her journal about light. Friends talked about her art. A young art historian spoke about how she'd brought Mother her problems and how wise Mother had been. It must have been wonderful, having her as a mother, she said to me afterward. I couldn't help raising my eyebrows. Well, yes and no. Later in the afternoon, my friend Judy Johnson called me to ask how it had gone. She was sorry she hadn't been able to be there. Then she asked what I was going to do about all Mother's paintings and her journals—while I was living in California, Judy had become quite friendly with Mother and had read a part of them. I hadn't thought about it. The paintings were stacked in warehouses, the journal manuscript was on Mother's desk. "Mother couldn't find a publisher for it, you know," I mumbled. "It needs editing." I was stalling. Finally, I said, "I'll do it if you'll help me." I knew Judy would defend Mother from me, she'd keep me fair.

For the next six years we worked on it together. Every time I made a trip to New York to visit my brother and later Lisa, who was then in graduate school at Columbia studying comparative literature, I visited Judy in her huge rambling house in Albany. I'd change into sweatpants to avoid the dog hairs that were all over the furniture, and she'd read over the commentary I'd written and defend Mother's actions. "Of course your mother wanted to have someone with her all the time," Judy would say, when Mother, refusing to be alone for even two minutes, insisted on having two servants, as well as a cook, rapidly depleting her capital and worrying my brother. "Remember, she had two serious falls. She couldn't get out of bed by herself. Think how helpless she must have felt."

"All right," I'd say. "All right." Then we'd spend half the night talking about Judy's poems and the autobiographical novel I was writing—and about our previous marriages. Judy, like me, had gotten out of a bad marriage. She hadn't wanted to leave Jimmy or to get the job teaching at the State University of New York, but having done both things she was flourishing. When I read her new poems, I saw a strong current of emotion I hadn't seen before. She had always had a formal brilliance; now, pain-soaked, her poems hit close to the bone. She had become a strong feminist, taught in both the Women's Studies and the English departments, and was a source of support for women struggling to find their voices. With me, though, she'd always been somewhat ambivalent—when we put on a show of Mother's work at SUNY, for instance, she told a local journalist that we were rivals, not friends—and I felt it was time to change this. I loved and admired her, but I didn't need to be put down anymore. We were giving a paper together at the City University of New York on our editing of Mother's journal. It was to be a dialogue between us. I had my part written out, but she wanted to improvise. Uneasy, I asked her to write hers out too. "This is ridiculous," I told her when I read it. "How can you say you had to give me permission to think my mother's art was important, that I had put her journals away in the cellar like some sort of junk. You make me sound like a fool. I hesitated to edit the journals not because I didn't think they were good but because I have such mixed feelings about my mother."

"Oh," Judy said, "I'm sorry." This was an important moment for me. Afterward, I stopped seeing Judy so much as a goddess, but more as a particularly gifted, fascinating human being. After that, things went better between us. At the conference, she made generous if slightly patronizing remarks about my coming out from under my mother's shadow and growing as an artist, and later she read a draft of my novel, commented warmly, and invited me up to SUNY for a reading.

In the fall of 1993, Mother's journal, *Hungry for Light,* and my novel, *Sins of the Mothers,* had a twin birth. When I read from the journal at Cody's bookstore in Berkeley, with my commentary and slides of Mother's paintings, people cried—I was almost crying myself. Her paintings were so luminous, her lyricism poignant, marvelous. I admired her spirit, the way she transcended her pain. I believed her when she said art should be gentle, beautiful, like the ancient art of China or Egypt, excluding everything ugly or angry. Yes, I found myself saying, yes.

Someone asked me afterward how I could have written a novel in which this eloquent, moving woman—clearly the basis for the fictional artist-mother—is portrayed as a monster of narcissism. Maybe some day I'll try to explain it, I told her. About how Mother is split. About how my feelings toward her are split, too. So far apart that I had to put one set of them in one book and one in another. I can't tell you now, I said, it's too complicated.

Before Mother died, I came close to her, but the past still unrolled behind me in two separate strands. In one, Mother is the gifted woman who taught me to love beauty and persevere in trying to create it, and in the other the raving, cruel woman who often hurt me. I still hadn't brought these two together and laid them to rest. It was hard to see Mother as one person; she flickered back and forth like those illustrations of figure and ground that you see first one way, then another.

Since writing is the way I learn things, I decided to write a novel about her as a young artist. I'd start from where I could still understand her imaginatively and try to figure out what made her the way she was later, what her own mother must have been like. What it was like growing up with a crazy brother. I began to think about how what we call a self is formed. What is it? What helps or hinders its growth? I imagined a spectrum of selves from the most rudimentary and damaged—an autistic child who can't even say the word *I*—to the most integrated, a healer, perhaps someone like Muriel. I put my young artist somewhere in the middle, like one of those countries with a highly developed north and an underdeveloped south.

I had also been thinking about Muriel. Her daughter, Connie, had written me around the time of Mother's death that Muriel had died suddenly of lung cancer. Connie wanted me to send memories or photos for a book she was planning. I had in mind an image of Muriel talking animatedly, with her lip drawn back crookedly on one side, a cigarette in her mouth. I started looking through my photo albums of the farm for pictures, but found surprisingly that there weren't many. There was one of her at a barbecue, her hair long, another riding a horse.

After my novel and Mother's journal came out, I realized I'd like to write about Muriel too, not a memoir but a fiction. Muriel wasn't just someone I loved. She was a model for life that I had had in front of my eyes but never used; I wanted to use it now. Most people have areas that are unused or split off, but with Muriel, I had the sense of a personality vibrantly whole to its outmost boundaries. I had rarely written about strong, loving people. Now I wanted to try—to set Muriel in a fictional context with my mother and my grandmother and my crazy uncle, and see what she would do with them. Maybe I could find new ways of looking at them myself. My novel *Paradise Farm* was the result. The great thing about being human is that you can recreate yourself, not by analyzing but by active imagining. A difficult family isn't fate. It dawned on me that I was beginning to hope again. I'd really forgotten how, ever since my father died, but now with Ira hope was growing back, like a severed nerve after an operation. I wanted to go forward into life and make things that had beauty, and love Ira and my children without so much fear.

That didn't mean that everything suddenly became easy. Ira and I saw the marriage counselor together on and off, learning to listen to each other's grievances. At a certain point Ira said it was enough. He'd had a realization, he told me. If he wanted this marriage—and he did—he was just going to have to do what it took to make it work. And I was going to have to do it too. It was as simple as that. A matter of attitude. Half the battle had been with himself, he said. It made sense. You can have insight up the wazoo and still do everything wrong. We knew what we should be doing. How not to pour oil on the flames of a minor discontent and how to smooth it down. How to negotiate disagreements. How to go easy on each other's sore points. The kind of support we each craved: the food, the lovemaking, the empathetic listening, the touching, the gifts. We weren't either of us easy people to satisfy— I know I wasn't once I took the lid off my suppressed desires—but we could read each other's signals the way a blind person reads braille. Let's stop talking about what we're going to do and just do it, Ira said. I must have looked skeptical because he took me in his arms. "Don't worry," he said, "risk free, money back if you're not satisfied. And to make it even more appealing, I'll start: Will you marry me?"

"We're already married," I said.

"But would you, if we weren't? I'm asking you again."

"I worry," I said, snuggling my head into his shoulder, "that you'll want to turn me in for a new model."

"Never," he said. "Unless your bottom rusts." He laughed at his metaphor, "You're high maintenance, but you're worth it. Am I worth it?"

"Oh, yes," I said, laughing with him.

"See, we can even laugh about being abandoned," he said. "We're making progress."

Epilogue

It's 1997, almost a new century. Ira and I have been together nearly seventeen years. We are waiting at the Rome airport for my son, Michael, and his wife, Monique Prieto, to arrive for a week's visit. Becca is going to come in a few days with her boyfriend, Andy. Two years ago, Alex came with Linda, his companion of ten years, and when they got back home, they decided to get married. One of the nice things about coming to Rome every spring is that it makes a nice destination for children and friends. And for us, it's perfect. Ira, after finishing a major work—*A History of Islamic Societies* for Cambridge University Press—has taken early retirement. He says he got the idea from looking at me and my kids doing things we like. From the time he was thirteen and worked in his father's cigar store in Brooklyn after school, he'd been watching the clock, making a career, never slacking off. Now he relaxes. He has discovered a talent for photography. He has taken up the violin again—a boyhood passion of his—and we joke that one day he'll go out in the piazza with it and pass the hat. Now the plane is late, and I pace up and down impatiently. Ira makes repeated trips to the announcement board. "It says 'landing,'" he tells me kindly. "Don't worry. You're not going to miss them." He's been saying that for the last half hour.

Finally Monique comes out with the baby, Emmet, in a baby pack on her chest and little Guillermo holding her hand. I hug her and then Guillermo, who looks like a blond Botticelli angel, and hear his sleepy whisper, low and sweet like a caress—hello, Grandma Brenda, hello, Grandpa Ira. I sneak a look at Emmet who is blissfully asleep. His hair has gotten lighter: it was jet black when he was born. After his birth I went down and helped out for a week, cooking and straightening and most of all playing with Guillermo, who was slightly shell-shocked by the new arrival. Emmet opens his eyes and looks straight at me; his eyes are a startling dark blue. Their baggage has been left behind in London, Monique says, and Michael is filling out forms. She is serene as always, and I think as I always do when I see her how lucky Michael is to have found this woman.

Their wedding in the Santa Monica Mountains at the ranch home of a friend, Anthony Duquette, set the tone for a marriage in which family is central, but beauty and style are there, too. Their friend Tony is a set designer and his ranch was filled with buildings and sculptures that he collected from all over the world, mostly Asia. For their wedding he made them a golden pavilion with a flagstone terrace bordered with trees, facing the mountains. Monique's mother was skeptical at first about having the wedding at Tony's. The road up the mountain was long and tortuous and she was afraid people would drive off a cliff coming back down late at night. The logistics of getting food and drink up there for two hundred guests were also awesome—not to speak of the cost. But Michael and Monique quietly insisted that this was what they wanted; they were artists. And Monique's mother came around, graciously, warmly, and helped them work it out. Tony, a man in his eighties, had gotten himself ordained so that he could marry them himself, and he was dressed in a gold-embroidered robe with an elaborate tall hat like a wizard in some enchanted fairy tale. The wedding itself was a riot of color: the groom's party in red jackets, the bridesmaids, who included Becca and Lisa, in gold dresses, Monique radiant in white. Her ninety-five-year-old grandma in hot pink.

Monique's family is a complicated but surprisingly harmonious mix. Both her parents have married again—her mother several times—and besides her grandma there was an assortment of stepparents, half-brothers, and uncles and aunts at the wedding. Monique's mother and stepmother have become best friends; they posed together, her mother's dark head next to her stepmother's blonde one, both with moist eyes. Monique's half-sister Brittany was the flower girl.

I am impressed by the way this family, several times fractured, has knit together again in a new form. I see the enveloping warmth that gives Michael such pleasure. Her family, Mexican in origin—with an admixture of Aztec Indian that would have made D. H.

Lawrence green with envy—has already absorbed an English woman and a midwesterner; they take Michael in easily, too. Our Jewishness becomes part of an American blend. "We were getting too inbred," I told Monique. Our family was too neurotic, I'm thinking, like show dogs. "You're bringing new blood into the family. It's great. I love it."

Richard was at the wedding, too, and he talked to me for the first time since our divorce. "I don't even recognize your voice," he told me, "you've become so, so . . ." He paused groping for a word. "Aggressive."

"Good," I said. "I'm glad I seem different." He asked me to pose for a picture with him and Michael. Later, I called him up and asked him if we couldn't start talking again like civil adults—I'd gotten my anger off my chest with my novel—but now he was angry and hurt. He said no, he had nothing more to say. I haven't given up on it, though. Monique's family is such a good example of how people can forgive each other.

Finally Michael comes out of customs looking tired but glad to be in Rome, and takes the baby from Monique. I love seeing how at ease he is with both children. Now he throws the baby up in the air and laughs. If Richard had thrown Michael like that I would have been terrified, but now I'm not even faintly worried. I know Michael knows what he is doing. He will catch Emmet.

The next day we have lunch out on our terrace surrounded by pink geraniums and vines and olive trees and flowering trees. Monique nurses Emmet often; he never cries. And when Guillermo gets edgy or jealous, she and Michael seem endlessly tolerant. Even when Guillermo is bouncing around on the couch next to Emmet and looks as if he might accidentally step on him, they stay cool, or they quietly remind him, no shoes on the bed. There is never any hint in their tone that Emmet might be in danger from his brother. They let Guillermo hold him on his lap, bring him things like stones or leaves, cover him with his blanket. As a result, Guillermo is developing a tenderness along with his rivalry: he holds Emmet's hand and asks him if he's happy now. Their way of handling things seems so much better than my mother's repeated, "Of course you hate your brother." And though I'd never said anything like that to my children, I'd made other mistakes. I'd assumed it was traumatic to have a sibling, and when Lisa insisted that she loved her baby brother, I never made any effort to let her express her negative feelings safely. It was either all bad or all okay. I hadn't been able to take an easy middle ground.

"Is Emmet lost?" Guillermo asks hopefully when Monique has covered Emmet's carriage with a blanket and he can't see him.

"No, he's not lost," she says.

"Why?" Guillermo asks. "Why isn't he lost?"

"Because we love both our boys," Monique says. "We would never lose either of them."

The way they do it, it all seems so easy. It's the same with other things too. The conflict between being an artist and being a mother, for instance. Monique is a gifted painter, an Abstract Expressionist who, in an almost uncanny coincidence, takes off from artists like Ellsworth Kelly, Mother's friend in the 1950s. She and Michael share the child care—though after Emmet's birth, they agreed that Michael needed more time to work at his music. But he still does the cooking—he has become an innovative cook. Last time I visited them in Los Angeles, he let me help prepare some particularly virulent red peppers for a Mexican chicken he was making. On Mother's Day he cooked dinner for Monique and her whole family. As a team, Michael and Monique manage what neither of them could do alone. She works at her art, he at his composition. Now he tells me that he has written the music for a film that will premier at the Venice Biennale in a few days. Monique will have shows next year in London and New York and L.A.

Unlike my mother, she has a refreshingly unpretentious attitude about her rather remarkable success. The art world is fickle, she says; today they like me, tomorrow they may not. The main thing is to keep working. Her work has wit as a central element. She plays with the traditions of the older generation of artists—making her paint drip upside down, for instance, or at improbable angles, making her flat shapes interact in amusing ways, giving her works irreverent titles. She seems to be saying, look here, art doesn't have to be tragic or dead serious. It can be fun. It's only coincidence, I know, but she seems like the antidote to my family myth of artistic gloom, madness, and suicide. She is the living proof that you can be a good artist and a good mother at the same time and be full of joy as well. She and Michael have painted their house in

Los Angeles all the colors of the rainbow: yellow bedrooms, the living room a ripe peach, the hall striped red and orange, the bathroom an electric green. It makes me smile every time I walk in the front door.

At the end of the week Becca arrives from Berkeley looking beautiful in a long flowered skirt and jeans vest. Her boyfriend, a musician, will join her later. She is tired but happy; she has just finished her last year of classes for a doctoral program in psychology. It's all done; she can hardly believe it; and she's gotten the internship she wanted for next year. In two years there'll be another Dr. R. Webster, she says, alluding to the degree she'll be getting. "Do you think they'll confuse me with Dad?"

"You can always use your middle name," I tell her. "Call yourself 'R. G.'"

She has been working with schizophrenics in a hospital. I think she is heroic the way she keeps on with this difficult, demanding work. Holding group sessions, actually getting these very disturbed people to talk not only to her but to one another. She tells me how she has done her first neuropsychological workup with a patient and has made a differential diagnosis. Now she is deeply concerned about this patient, wonders what her diagnosis will mean for his life. I suppress the thought that he is in such bad shape, it won't really matter much. But this isn't the point. What is important is the degree of her caring. It's this quality that must get through to her patients and make them—even the violent, supposedly hopeless ones—respond to her. How different from Maenchen with her sighs and barely restrained impatience.

"You should go back into therapy for a while," Becca tells me. "Talk to someone about all the bad therapy you've had."

"I don't really want to," I tell her. "I've had enough. I'd rather think about it myself."

Becca sometimes carries Emmet, sometimes I do, sometimes Ira as we go around Rome together. We stop in a rose garden on the Aventine Hill and lie on the grass. The roses are in full bloom, pink and red. Bees are everywhere, but they are busy with the flowers and don't bother us. We slip off our shoes and look at the cypresses in the distance against the sky. It is an almost perfect moment. As perfect as you can get in this life, but I miss Lisa. I wish she were here with us.

A few weeks earlier I saw her in New York as I was leaving for Rome. We struggled for the millionth time over my faults as a mother during her adolescence, but this time something finally clicked. I got it. I understood that my attitudes, my panic and anger, had made her feel bad about herself. Over dim sum at a Thai restaurant, I told her how sorry I was, and this time I think she believed me. We went shopping together for clothes for her birthday. "You know," I told her, after we'd bought a pair of designer black leather pants that fit her like a second skin and set off her newly orange hair, "when you love someone, you tend to feel they are like you. I realize now that you are different."

"That's what I've been trying to tell you for so long," she says. A few years earlier her graduate studies had ceased to interest her and she'd given them up. She learned desktop publishing and eventually found an interesting job as managing editor of an on-line art journal. I thought of how many years it had taken me to fight free of my mother. It's not easy being a firstborn daughter. Good for her. She was going to do it sooner. We looked at ourselves in the mirror, me in my conventional linen suit, her, hip and gorgeous and slim, denizen of another world—a world of models and artists, of spectacle and fierce play and staying out in your favorite club till morning.

"You really are different," I repeated, "but I still love you very much. Who is to say that your choices aren't just as good, even better than mine? Who am I to preach marriage and children to you? Look how unhappy I was for such a long time. You've made a life for yourself, interesting work, plenty of friends." I paused, suppressing the wish that my beautiful, talented daughter had someone— man or woman, I'd stopped long ago thinking it had to be a man— who valued her as she deserved to be valued. Even though I wanted more than anything else for her to be fulfilled and happy, it wasn't my business any more. She was the one who had to engineer her own happiness. Not her linen-suited, to-bed-at-ten Mommy. Now in Rome, Becca tells me that Lisa is in love with someone wonderful. A woman who is not only a good person but a strong and highly successful one. I e-mail Lisa that I am happy for her and she e-mails back that finally she's found someone everyone will be able to get along with, including herself. Maybe next year she'll come to Rome.

On the last day of Becca's visit—Andy went home earlier—she gets an attack of feeling dizzy and curls up in bed in Ira's green-and-white striped pajamas. They are too short for her and we laugh. Ira asks her if she thinks she could eat a pizza, and when she says yes, he goes down to the corner and brings some upstairs and we sit around her bed trying not to drop the thin-crusted, tomato-laden slices. Becca revives; she asks Ira questions about Italian history. Afterward, she wants to go over the family history, to hear the story of how she and each of her siblings were born. She wants to know what they looked like, how I fed them. We go on talking into the night. The moon is out over our terrace. Moonlight filters softly in through the open door. I pat Becca's leg, thinking how beautiful she is with her dark serious eyes and fine blonde hair. She is listening intently to me as I describe how fiercely she sucked as a baby. How determined you were even then, I say. You were just going to get every last drop. We laugh.

I feel sorry for my mother's never having had this, never having nursed or changed me or Chris, never even having had the joy of talking intimately with us—stuck on the treadmill of her endless analysis with Dr. Kris, worrying her past like a dirty bone. It could have happened to me, but I was lucky. I escaped. I got another chance at life. Lucky in my children too. How they kept me anchored when they were small. How with all my errors they've grown and flourished. Becca falls asleep, a little smile on her face. I sit and watch her until the morning birds begin their first inquiring calls.